WOMBAT

WOMBAT

By C.K. Thompson, R.A.O.U., J.P.
(Member of the Royal Zoological Society of N.S.W. and the
Royal Australasian Ornithologists' Union)

This edition published 2017
By Living Book Press
147 Durren Rd, Jilliby, 2259
Copyright © The Estate of C.K. Thompson, 1940

The publisher would like to give a huge 'Thank You' to the author's family for their
assistance in making this book available once more.

ISBN: 978-0-6481048-6-5

CONTENTS

AUTHOR'S NOTE

Although the wombat has been described often as the surliest and grumpiest animal in the Australian bush, this is really a slander on one of our most interesting marsupials. Wombats may look bad-tempered and stupid and may be unsociable in their wild state, but people who have reared them from cubhood as pets, report that in captivity, they are affectionate, inoffensive, playful and amusing

There are many well-authenticated stories of pet wombats wandering in and out of houses like dogs, following children around like ordinary domestic animals, sleeping in armchairs and even enjoying to be nursed like a baby—a rather tough—looking and hefty baby when fully grown!

First record of a wombat seems to have been made in 1797 when the ship *Sydney Cove* was wrecked on an island in Bass Strait. There were plenty of wombats around, and the shipwrecked crew lived on them until rescued by the ship *Francis*, which took a sample wombat back to Sydney for Governor Hunter to have a look at. He thought it was such a novelty that he sent it home to England with a letter stating that the aboriginals called it "wombach." The Governor also wrote that from its burrowing habits it was thought to be a species of badger, but it also had the same manners as a bear.

Unlike a number of Australian animals and birds, the wombat has the distinction of retaining its aboriginal name. Early white settlers called it either beaver or badger—and it bears not the faintest resemblance to either. The pioneers named many of our native creatures after those they had seen in England and Europe. For instance, they called the Tasmanian marsupial wolf "hyena," the koala "bear," the dasyures "native cats," and the spiny ant-eater "porcupine." They also called the piping crow-shrike "magpie." I prefer "magpie."

The pioneers and bushmen ate wombats when they ran out of other meat. Opinions vary as to the eating qualities of "badger steaks," but one well-known naturalist has stated that had wombat been first-class "tucker" instead of tasting musky and being very sinewy, the pioneers would have cleaned up every one and thus caused the early extinction of a notable marsupial.

Wombats are not very popular with farmers and settlers, because they break down wire netting fences to get at vegetable crops, while their long, deep tunnels constitute a danger to stock, and provide rabbits with ready-made warrens and burrows.

There are four kinds of wombats, two having hairy noses and two being "clean-shaven." Naked Nose prefers hilly forest and coastal country, while Hairy Nose inhabits the drier inland areas. Though all species were once very plentiful throughout Australia, Tasmania and the Bass Strait islands, gradually they are becoming fewer, and the day may arrive when they will become extinct. It is to be hoped that enough will be preserved in sanctuaries and reservations to obviate this zoological tragedy.

It is of great interest to note in passing that at Mowbray Swamp near Smithton in the north-west corner of Tasmania, scientists recently found the remains of a wombat the size of a pony. This gigantic "badger" and his relatives roamed the countryside about 600,000 years ago during the Ice Age.

An old bushman friend of mine once told me that wombats are so short-sighted that they will walk right past a man and not see him. Perhaps they don't want to see him. Maybe they are a little particular about the company they keep! This old chap also told me that when a wombat crosses a river or creek he just walks under the water "because he can't swim like a wallaby does." You cannot beat old bushmen for telling tall stories, can you? He did not tell me how many of these aquatic wombats got stuck in the mud and never saw their burrows again!

Though the wombat has been relentlessly persecuted by the white man from the earliest days because of its destructive habits, it is, like the platypus, the spiny ant-eater and the shy little numbat, a wholly distinctive Australian and, as such, should never be allowed to become extinct.

C. K. THOMPSON

CHAPTER ONE

The Coming of Bill

H IGH up among the rocks on the side of a steep hill which was one of a chain forming an insignificant spur of the Great Dividing Range, an old wombat had sunk a deep shaft and had made it her home. She was not unique in that. The hillside was honeycombed with similar burrows, in each of which dwelt a wombat, keeping strictly to itself.

Except in the mating season, which lasted only a few months—from round about April to June—they were an unsociable lot, these wombats. When they were not hunting for food, which generally was after night had fallen, they lodged deep in their burrows, receiving no visitors and paying no social calls. They were not, however, strictly nocturnal. On occasions they moved around in the daylight, but had absolutely no truck with each other, whether it was morning, noon or night. Their only relaxation appeared to be an occasional sunbath, taken in a shallow depression scooped out of the earth against a log or a rock. Almost every burrow that housed a wombat had its adjacent "bath." But some of the marsupials were so reserved and aloof that they did not even indulge in the luxury of a sunbake lest some other wombat, or perhaps a passing snake or twittering bird should observe them and thus disturb their privacy.

The old female wombat had sunk her burrow into the hillside several years earlier. The ground was so hard that she had driven the tunnel only a dozen feet, but the circumference was capacious enough for a child to crawl into if any child had the temerity to do so. Some of her neighbours who had tunnelled into softer earth had sunk their shafts to greater depths, the longest being almost fifty feet.

The old wombat, stoutly-built, clumsy-looking, with a short broad muzzle and thick, short stout limbs, clad in a coarse brown furred coat, had furnished her burrow with a very comfortable nest of bark, grass and leaves, which was located at the extremity in a small chamber she had hollowed out.

And it was here that her son Bill was born. He was a rather unattractive morsel of wombathood, was Bill. Skinny and hairless, he gave no hint in his early days of the powerful animal into which he would grow—provided always that the perils of the bush did not overtake him and shorten the life span that Mother Nature had intended for him.

Bill was an only child. It was a very rare thing for a wombat to have more than one youngster at a time, and Bill's mother conformed to the accepted practice of her race. For some months he was content to dwell in his mother's pouch, but when he was six months old and was fully furred, he was informed, politely but firmly, that his mother intended resigning her position as a convenient method of transport, and from then on he could get around on his own legs.

Bill did not object to this. He was growing fast and in due course would construct his own burrow and set up his home. He was no mother's boy.

From the mouth of the burrow a well-defined path led down to the open country where there was plenty of sweet green grass and Bill and his mother made nightly excursions there for food. But they did not exist on grass alone. The inner bark of trees, roots of shrubs, thistles and similar herbage were frequent items on the menu. When Bill was very young, his mother often sought out patches of swordgrass and, pulling the stems out singly, gave them to Bill so that he could feast upon the soft white base-ends.

During their quests for food, they saw other wombats, but passed them as if they did not exist. On one occasion, a tough old man wombat deliberately barged into Bill, who was not quick enough to get out of his path. Bill resented this, and expressed his resentment with a few hoarse grunts; but his mother passed the matter over lightly. She succeeded in conveying to her son the information that the old man wombat had not been aggressive or looking for trouble, neither had he been particularly discourteous. He had been merely observing the wombat practice of keeping rigidly aloof from his kinsfolk. He just had not seen Bill. Privately, Bill thought that this was carrying unsociability to the extreme even if, like most wombats, the old warrior had been short-sighted.

It was when Bill was not quite twelve months old that he witnessed an unprecedented episode.

He and his mother were lumbering along a path towards the feeding grounds one night when they met another wombat. It was a large male and Bill got out of its path, expecting it to pass by without recognition. Judge his surprise, then, when it stopped and gave a hoarse grunt of greeting. This was astounding enough in itself, but when his own mother, his friend and guide who had taught him never to associate with others of his species, affectionately returned the greeting, Bill was, in turn, amazed, disgusted and perturbed.

The strange wombat advanced slowly until its nose actually rubbed that of Bill's mother. This was it, Bill told himself. She would never stand for that type of funny business. He looked at her in anticipation, confident that she would bite the impudent nose clean off the offensive newcomer. But when she rubbed her cheek against that nose instead of nipping it off, Bill was quite dumbfounded. In his limited experience, there was absolutely no precedent for that kind of thing.

Now thoroughly disgusted, the young wombat mooched away by himself, following the track that his mother and her new boy friend had taken, but proceeding slowly so as not to catch up with them. Obviously they were making for the usual feeding ground, and Bill, too, wanted to go there.

It was the only good browsing patch he knew and though he might feel indignant at his mother's betrayal of the wombat code of solitude, his indignation was not deep enough to put him on a hunger-strike.

In due course he reached the grassland, a fairly wide expanse of country bountifully grassed with luscious herbage, through which a shallow creek sang and babbled its way to join the river many miles to the south.

When Bill arrived, he noticed that there were several other wombats at dinner, but he took no notice of them. He could not see his mother or her new friend, and far from feeling hurt about it, was pleased.

He spent most of the night browsing on the grass or lying around loafing, and an hour or so before dawn decided to return home. Then it occurred to him that he did not have a home. Oh, yes, there was the burrow previously occupied by him and his mother, but he did not feel inclined to stay there any more. He would have either to find a disused one or dig one for himself. Pondering the pros and cons as he trotted along, he decided to spend one last day in the family tunnel and on the following night to find a new residence and to live a free and independent bachelor existence.

Reaching the old familiar tunnel, he was about to slip into it when he met with a sudden check. Just inside the entrance with his nose poking out, was the strange wombat that his mother had befriended. Bill looked at him scornfully and then, over this animal's head, noticed his own mother. The look she gave her son was far from friendly, but this meant nothing. His mother would not have been an honest-to-goodness wombat if she had looked friendly.

Bill eyed the stranger with dislike and attempted to push past him to get into the burrow. The stranger, however, stood four-square and contested the move. His attitude was quite plain—Bill was not welcome. The stranger was a large and powerful animal and made its meaning and attitude perfectly clear by rearing on its haunches and bringing its heavy front paws down hard on Bill's head.

Withdrawing and mustering up all his dignity, Bill threw a glance of withering scorn at the wombat and another at his mother. Then he wheeled around and lumbered away. As this was wombat country he did not anticipate any difficulty in finding a temporary home. There was certain to be disused burrows around. In this his confidence was justified, for he had to go only a few hundred yards before he came upon a deep tunnel which bore every sign of being deserted.

He crawled into it and proceeded confidently. That it had been disused for some considerable time was apparent by the small falls of earth. Eventually he reached the end and though the nest of bark and dried grass was very old and definitely second hand, it would do him for one sleep, he decided.

Bill slept for a few hours and then woke up. He was

not comfortable and did not feel at home. He was restless and a little unhappy. For a time he lay in the old nest and then, getting up, made his way up the burrow to the open air. Outside the sun was shining brightly and it made him blink. He emerged from the tunnel and spent half an hour in a nearby dusthole before returning to the burrow to catch up on his sleep.

Bill used his new home for a week—seven long days and nights of restlessness, tinged with unhappiness. He did not know what was wrong with him, but he did know one thing—the charm of that district had gone.

He was returning from the grasslands very early one spring morning when he reached a great decision—he would leave this district and make his home elsewhere in some faraway place. As to his present temporary abode, he would not sleep in it again.

And though he did not relish travelling in broad daylight, the urge to depart was so great that he had to obey it. So off he went—lumbering aimlessly away on a trail that might lead to anywhere.

CHAPTER TWO

Bush Revenge

HAVING no immediate locality in view and not caring how much time he spent on house-hunting, Bill had not gone very far before he decided to have a rest, so he selected a shallow depression near a big log. This was open forest country, and there were several shallow depressions in the vicinity, apparently dustholes belonging once to grey kangaroos.

The signs told Bill that the kangaroos had not been around for some considerable time. These big marsupials were nomadic in their habits, wandering around the countryside in disorganised mobs, generally without an acknowledged leader. Their home was where they happened to be and the mob that had frequented the district where Bill now was, was many miles away.

Dropping into the dusty depression with a tired grunt, Bill was content to allow the rest of the bush to go hang, but from the activity all around him, he was the only lazy creature in those parts. It was early spring, and therefore nesting and breeding time for most of the birds and animals.

Lying negligently on his back in the dusthole, his short limbs pointing lazily skywards, Bill's attention was attracted to a large handsome bird perched on the limb of a tree directly over his head. It was a red goshawk, a rather rare bird of prey, and it was looking at Bill as if it resented his being there. Actually, the red goshawk was not interested at all in Bill. It had seen him arrive and take up quarters in the kangaroo's disused dust-bath, and as long as he stayed there, the red goshawk was quite satisfied. Not that the handsome bird had anything to fear from the dumpy, earth-bound wombat.

The red goshawk was waiting for something to turn up in the way of prey. Its nest was half a mile away in a tall ironbark and was being looked after by its mate who, in addition, had two lusty nestlings to care for. It was not long since these young ones had emerged from their lavender-marked, bluish-white eggs and the parent red goshawks were hard put to it to sate the appetites of their vigorous offspring. Their visits to and from their large nest of sticks lined with leaves were many and the distances they had to travel with food grew longer as the supply nearer to home diminished.

Birds, reptiles and small animals formed the main diet of the red goshawks and the pair of birds had absolutely ter-rorised the neighbourhood ever since their youngsters had emerged from the eggs. Nothing was safe from or sacred to them. Their repeated raids on the nests of other birds had decimated the immediate vicinity of their own nest and the red goshawks had been forced to exist on mice and lizards with grasshoppers for dessert. They got along more or less satisfactorily, their fierce hooked bills making short work of any hapless creature captured.

At the exact moment that the male red goshawk sat in the tree over Bill the wombat's head, there was only one nest with nestlings in the area, and that belonged to a pair of magpies. There were three large fledglings in it and the red goshawk had been trying to make up his mind for days to attack it. He was not afraid of the magpies, but he had enough sense to realise that tackling those indomitable birds would be a different proposition from raiding the nest of a peewit or a willy wagtail.

Not that peewits were easy game. The red goshawk and his mate together had attacked the nest of one pair and had been met with fierce opposition by the peewits, who were determined to protect their large mud nest by every means in their power. They gave the red goshawks a rough time, but unfortunately it was not rough enough—the hawks each had got away with a nestling. Nothing daunted, the valiant black and white birds had mated again and there were three new eggs in their mud home. The red goshawk knew this, but eggs did not interest him as much as nestlings, and he was content to wait until they hatched out.

But peewits and magpies were alike only in colouring. In fighting prowess, the magpie could lick half a dozen peewits. There were very few birds in the bush that could handle a magpie even at ordinary times; while in the nesting season, the sharp-billed magpie was a fighting fury that was given a wide berth by all sensible birds.

The red goshawk knew all about this. It did not scare him but it did make him cautious. He was as game as any magpie ever hatched, but was not silly enough to attack the pied songsters' nest while the owners were in residence.

Sitting on the limb over the wombat's head, the red goshawk turned the matter over and over in his mind. The tree containing the magpies' nest was only a hundred yards away and he could see it from where he sat. It was a large structure of sticks and it was continually guarded by one or other of the parent birds. That was the whole trouble from the red goshawk's point of view. In ordinary circumstances, both birds would be out hunting for food for their hungry children, but the presence of the red goshawks in the neighborhood—which of course was well known to the magpies—made it imperative that the nest be not left unguarded for a moment.

The red goshawk had flown unobtrusively into the tree where he was now perched and, as far as he knew, the magpies were unaware of it. He based his belief on the fact that he had remained unmolested. He felt quite sure that had the magpies sighted him they would have given battle at once. He was sorry now that he had not brought his mate with him. One of them might have been able to create a diversion to enable the other to attack the nest.

But what guarantee had he that even that plan would work? As far as that went, he could not be certain of the outcome of an attack launched on the nest by him and his mate in concert. It was a worrying problem, no question about it.

And so the red goshawk sat there in the tree hoping that both magpies would leave the nest long enough for him to raid it and secure one or more of the fledglings.

His prayers, suddenly, were answered. One of the magpies which had been away hunting, returned to the nest with a morsel and was greeted eagerly by the squawking youngsters. The row they kicked up yelling for food made the red goshawk's bill water. The parent magpie stayed only long enough to pop the tid-bit into a gaping mouth and then was off again—but this time was followed by its mate, who wanted a bit of exercise.

On silent wings the red goshawk plunged straight at the magpies' nest but had not covered half the distance before the harsh screech of a peewit rent the air and two gallant little black and white birds darted from their own nest nearby to intercept the fleeting hawk. The warning cry of the peewits reached the two magpies, who wheeled round like jet fighters piloted by war aces and came back like a pair of arrows.

The peewits reached the magpies' nest a second ahead of the red goshawk and with shrill cries and beating wings sought to divert the red terror from the fledglings. The red goshawk did not land on or near the nest, but shot straight over it, deliberately barging into a peewit and knocking the spirited little bird head over claws in midair. It righted itself and flew uncertainly to a nearby branch to recover its equilibrium, while its small mate flew round and round the red goshawk, harassing it, insulting it, but doing it little harm.

And then the angry parent magpies hurtled into the fray. The red goshawk was big and it was a fierce fighter. It wheeled after its encounter with the peewit and was ready for both magpies. Those enraged birds, disdaining finesse in battle, dashed at the intruder with snapping beaks and beating wings, and feathers flew in all directions as three irate birds fought in the air, among the branches and around the nest.

The undamaged peewit flew on the outskirts of the battle excitedly endeavouring to take part, while its flustered little mate perched on a nearby tree limb and carefully examined itself for injuries. Finding none, it, too, took to the air and tried to enter the fight, but like its mate it was forced into the unwilling role of onlooker.

What with the screeching of the red goshawk, the squawking of the magpies, the harsh, flat notes of the peewits and the excited chatter of an inquisitive willy wagtail which was looping the loop like an insane aeroplane pilot, the bush was turned into a pandemonium which effectually disturbed the rest of Bill the wombat. He could not see much of what was going on among the treetops, but he could hear it, and he wished heartily that those noisy birds would go elsewhere and do their ungentlemanly brawling.

But if the noise merely annoyed the wombat, it had a different effect upon the various birds in the area. To all the feathered creatures the red goshawk was a mortal enemy. Most of them had cause to rue the day that the bird of prey and his mate had made their home there. Willy wagtails, honeyeaters, apostle birds, finches of all kinds, butcher birds and several others, not content to be just bystanders, flashed from tree, bush and scrub to assist the battling magpies and their peewit auxiliaries. The peewits were the most recent sufferers, and they yearned to get to close quarters with the red goshawk. The magpies, however, gave them no space in which to operate.

It was, of course, nothing new for many different birds to combine in attacking a common enemy, but on this occasion there were so many of them that it had its advantages for the red goshawk. They got in each other's way and one magpie; to its surprise, found itself in a claw to claw bout with a pied butcher bird, while four apostle birds were engaged in a fierce struggle among themselves. And willy wagtail was most indignant when a peewit tried to pull out his tail-feathers.

The pied butcher bird that accidentally had become entangled with the magpie, had a nest in the fork of a high gum tree not far from the magpie's own home. It was an open and deep structure of sticks and twigs, lined with dried grass and fibre roots. At one stage it had contained five greyish-green eggs speckled with brown and these had mysteriously disappeared while the parent birds were out hunting one day. A passing crow had been responsible for the theft, but the butcher bird blamed the red goshawk and now sought a chance for revenge. He quickly disengaged himself from the magpie, with whom he had no quarrel at all, and added his flute-like notes to the general uproar.

Bird calls singly, and even collectively when in harmony, are a delight to hear, but when they are all mixed up in one squawking chorus, it can be nerve-wracking. So thought Bill the wombat, and he resolved to move away to try to find peace elsewhere.

But before he could put his resolve into action, things began to happen.

The red goshawk succeeded in disengaging himself from the fighting balls of feathers and, turning tail, fled swiftly away. This was the signal for all the other birds to cease their private quarrels and to take after him. The magpies, the peewits, the butcher bird and most of the lesser fry, willy wagtail well in front, formed up like a squadron of fighter planes and dive-bombed him relentlessly. He could not retain height and they forced him lower and lower until eventually he crash-landed—right on top of the startled wombat lying in his dusthole.

Scrambling to his feet with a loud grunt of surprise, Bill found himself the centre of a heap of fighting birds. The red goshawk was down on the ground now, valiantly endeavouring to beat off the combined assaults of his enemies, who were determined to do him as much harm as they could. Willy wagtail, nearly crazy with excitement, darted hither and thither above the feather mass without being able to lend a beak or claw and then perched on Bill's back, using him as a grandstand and chattering shrilly into his ear.

That, for Bill, was the final insult. He got under way and left the spot at a shambling trot, treading on the red goshawk as he did so. That wounded nest robber screeched loudly and for the first time the other birds became aware of

Bill's presence. With one accord they swept from the earth and vanished into various trees, while the red goshawk, bedraggled and with quite a few feathers missing, managed to become air-borne and, wobbling unsteadily, made its ragged way back to its own nest.

Grunting and snorting to himself, Bill the wombat ambled through the thickets, heading for nowhere in particular. High up in a spotted gum where they had flown after the defeat of the red goshawk, the magpies watched his departure with kindling eyes. The male bird decided that he did not like Bill and, launching himself from the tree, dived straight and true, his long, sharp bill striking Bill exactly where his tail would have been if he had one. Bill's startled grunt of wounded surprise echoed through the scrub and as the magpie whirled aloft and returned to his nest, the wombat bolted, more than effectually speeded upon his parting way.

As he mooched along, Bill told himself that he had only himself to blame. He had no right to be wandering around in the middle of the day. The sun shone warmly on his thick fur and he was hot, tired and thirsty. He managed to cool himself somewhat with a draught of murky water from a leaf-filled rock-pool, and then decided to find a place to sleep in. He did not like the idea of camping out in the open where he was liable to be disturbed by fighting birds, so he looked around for a place in which to dig a burrow—a permanent one if possible. He could not find a satisfactory site, but luck favored him by directing his dragging footsteps to a cleft in some rocks. It would do for a time. Let him have a good sleep and then he could find a permanent dwelling.

Bill was investigating the rock cleft when he was startled by a terrific screaming as if every bird in creation were holding a council meeting and objecting to something the

mayor had said. He snorted loudly and disgustedly, thinking
that the red goshawk and his enemies had followed him to
renew their hostilities, whereas the noise was created by a
flock of little green parakeets which flashed like miniature
verdant bullets through the leaves and branches overhead
so swiftly that the eye scarcely could follow them.

Bill did not try to follow them with his eye. Birds gave
him a pain in the neck and he had no wish to dislocate that
neck by attempting the impossible. In any case he was so
constructed by nature that he could not do any star-gazing
if he had wanted to.

His startled surprise quickly gave way to exasperation
as the parakeets, refusing to go away, dashed in and out of
the treetops, screaming shrilly as if they were being hunted
by some feathered Nemesis.

And they were. Bill learned this in tragic fashion when
something as soft as thistledown fell lightly on his back
and then tumbled to the ground. It was the dead body of
one of the little "greenies." Bill looked at it thoughtfully,
decided that it was no good to eat, and then resumed his
inspection of the rock cleft.

The unfortunate green parakeet had been a victim of
the swiftest member of the hawk family—a peregrine or
blackcheeked falcon—which even now was still chasing and
dealing out death to the frantic flock above. An absolute
demon, the falcon was the only bird of prey capable of following the incredibly swift-flying parakeets as they flashed
among twigs, branches and leaves, and killing them with
blows delivered with the hind claw during lightning-like
swoops. Bold and fearless to a high degree, there was hardly
a bird it would not tackle and even willy wagtail, who knew
more tricks than the greatest human stunt aeroplane pilot,
was not safe from it.

Finally, in an effort to rid themselves of the awful death-dealing slayer on their tails, the parakeets flew deeper into the bush and Bill the wombat was left in peace. He managed to enter the cleft in the rocks, though there was not much space to spare for his bulk, and settled down for a good sleep .

CHAPTER THREE

The Chinese Gardens

Two years had passed since Bill the wombat had left his mother's burrow. Where he had been born he did not now have the slightest recollection and he did not care a jot. He had some faint memories of a furry old mother and a deep tunnel in some rocky hills, but those were dim and distant days and not worth pondering on.

Now fully grown, Bill was a solemn-looking fellow and he always got around with a grumpy look on his muzzle as if the cares of the whole bush were upon his dumpy shoulders. A very powerful animal, his coarse, grey-brown furred coat covered a body which would weigh all of 80 lbs., he would measure something like three feet and a half from the tip of his rather blunt nose to the point where his tail would be if he possessed one. Not that anybody had ever tried to weigh Bill or to measure him, but those were the figures they would have got if they had done so.

Bill lived in a permanent burrow now. He had driven it deep into the side of a ridge which overlooked a picturesque expanse of agricultural land and his existence was more or less peaceful, though a rather unusual one. It was unusual in that Bill had unwilling human providers of nourishment;

and these humans themselves were a little unusual—Chinese market gardeners.

Around these hills and ridges were other wombats, but Bill had little to do with them. Like all his kind who lived solitary lives except in the mating season, Bill kept to himself. As to food, he was not very hard to please. Grass, the inner bark of certain trees, roots of shrubs and, of course, vegetables of all kinds from the Chinese gardens, suited his palate nicely.

Bill was a marsupial, but he differed from every other marsupial in one respect—all his teeth had no roots. Continuous growth, however, prevented them from being worn away through constant use.

And Bill had plenty of use for his teeth. When he selected the site of his present burrow—and he had now been occupying it for about two months—he did not search around for the easiest place to dig. On his feet he had nails which were like shovels and these, coupled with his powerful teeth, made burrow-excavating simple. Lying on his side, he went to work, tearing away the earth and stones with his front paws and pushing out the debris with his hind ones. When he came to a tough tree root he did not burrow round it, but gnawed it away with his teeth.

By nature and instinct, the wombat was now chiefly a creature of the night. During the daylight hours he remained deep inside his burrow, emerging after dark to prowl around and feed. There were, though, odd occasions when he ventured abroad in the daytime, but he did not make a habit of it.

Since he had left the parent burrow he had had several homes in various localities, but he regarded his latest residence as his permanent abode.

Bill's acquaintance with the Chinese market gardeners

began about a week after he had completed his burrow. He had been in the habit of feeding with other wombats, but not in their company, in various spots around the flats and the creek—which was some distance away—but one night he fossicked his way down the hillside and mooched across the wide flat until he found himself against a dilapidated fence with rusty old wire netting on it. He sniffed the netting suspiciously, and then ambled through it as if it were not there. A few yards inside the fence brought him to what he must have regarded as a wombat's heaven—a big patch of succulent lettuce.

Having dined superbly off lettuce, Bill proceeded leisurely through the well-kept gardens, pausing anon to detach a cabbage leaf, grab a mouthful of carrot top or make short work of a clump of spinach. He made regular nightly visits to the gardens after that and was left unmolested because nobody saw him.

One night about two weeks after he had first discovered the gardens, he was late in arriving, having first gone prospecting around the creek. It was a little unfortunate for him that he had reached the gardens so late, because dawn—and the Chinese—found him still poking around the vegetable beds.

Yet Yow, Hook Suey and Wu Wang saw this strange-looking animal making himself at home in their cabbages and stared at him in wild surmise. None of them had ever seen anything like Bill before and they hesitated about approaching him. Bill was a rugged-looking type with a wicked-looking eye. Definitely a tough character—on looks. How were the three yellow gentlemen to know that underneath his hard exterior, Bill was really a harmless, benevolent gentleman if left alone?

Bill saw the Chinese and looked them over, only partially

interested. He was not the least bit afraid of them, chiefly because he had had no previous contact with humans and, therefore, did not realise their capacity for doing him harm.

He emerged from the cabbage bed and stood on the path watching their cautious approach. Yet Yow, holding a hoe, Hook Suey armed with a spade and Wu Wang bearing a bucket, were ready for instant flight at the first hint of belligerence on the part of the wombat. They came to a halt at last and stood looking at him warily. Bill returned the look, but his interest was waning. He was feeling tired and was thinking that it was high time he turned in. So, keeping to the path, he toddled off the way he had come and in due course arrived at his burrow and bed.

Yet Yow, Hook Suey and Wu Wang held a conference and inspected the damage to the gardens. Their vegetable loss was small and that did not worry them much. They were more concerned over what had caused the damage. They had, of course, known for sometime that something had been raiding their gardens and now they had found out what it was, they were much puzzled.

Wu Wang ventured the opinion that it was a pig. Yet Yow reckoned it was a badger, pictures of which he had seen at some time or other. Hook Suey stoutly maintained that it was a beaver. He also had once read a picture book.

Still sticking to his pig theory, Wu Wang advanced the suggestion that it would make a nice meal. This made his friends lick their lips, because they all loved pork. Then Hook Suey threw a wet blanket on the idea by stating that if it were a pig, then somebody owned it and there would be trouble if they caught it and ate it.

The three Chinese were still pondering the puzzle as they worked diligently in their garden. Yet Yow, plying his hoe between two rows of beetroot, paused and, leaning on the handle, bent a mild glance on Hook Suey, who was digging up a plot of ground nearby.

"Badger," he said, speaking, of course, in his native tongue.

"No stripes on him. Wrong colour," said Hook Suey.

"Also wrong country. Badger in England, not Australia," said Wu Wang, who was pulling up weeds and throwing them into his bucket.

"Beaver," said Hook Suey, resuming his digging.

"No tail. Beaver has big flat tail. Also wrong country. Beaver in America, not Australia. Pig," said Wu Wang.

"No tail. Nose like rabbit. Pig has flat nose and curly tail," said Yet Yow, getting to work with the hoe.

"We will ask Sergeant Murphy. He will know," said Hook Suey.

"Sergeant Murphy knows only of thieves and criminals, not animals," objected Wu Wang.

"Policeman know everything about everything," said Hook Suey and they left it at that.

Some hours later when Hook Suey drove into the markets with a load of produce, he saw Sergeant Arthur Murphy in the street and, reining his placid old horse to a halt, raised a solemn hand in greeting. Sergeant Murphy, who was in his uniform as a mounted policeman, strolled across the footpath and greeted Hook Suey cheerfully.

"How is the price of bananas today, John?" he asked. It was a stock joke of the sergeant's, but the market gardener answered him gravely. "No glow banana. Cabbagee, lettucee, onion. You likee?"

"Not this morning, thank you," answered Murphy. "Anyway, did you want to see me about something?"

Hook Suey told him of the strange visitor to the gardens that morning and how he and his two companions had been unable to decide whether it was a pig, a badger or a beaver.

"From what you say, and the way you describe it, I'd say it was a wombat," said the sergeant.

"Lombat?" repeated the Chinese. "Is that Austlalian pig?"

"Definitely not," said Murphy. "A wombat is as much like a pig as soap is like concrete. Though I must say that in the early days the old bushmen thought they were wild pigs and used to eat them."

"Good to eat, huh?" asked Hook Suey eagerly. "Nicee like pig?"

"No, they are not," said the sergeant, wagging a finger at him. "They don't taste a bit like pork. I've had a go at them in my time and they taste awful. I'd rather eat an old boot myself."

"Velly dangelous animal?" asked the Chinese. "Bite hole in man?"

"No," laughed Murphy. "Wombats are as harmless as Chinamen." Hook Suey considered that for a time and seemed very doubtful.

"He look velly wild," he said seriously.

"Looks are not everything. If it is a wombat, don't you worry your pretty head over it, John. He might eat a few of your spring onions and things, but he won't bite you. Anyway, he might make a nice pet for you."

Bill no doubt would have been gratified to hear of this testimonial on his behalf issued by the police force, but Bill was sleeping peacefully in his burrow.

Hook Suey, on his return from the markets, faithfully reported the conversation to Yet Yow and Wu Wang, who were relieved to learn that they need fear no vicious and unprovoked assaults from Bill the wombat.

They did not see anything of him for some time after that, though they did see evidence of his visits in the shape of missing vegetables. Prospecting around, Yet Yow discovered the hole in the rusty wire and debated with his friends whether they should repair it. Bill had made so many trips to the gardens now that he had a faintly-worn track from his burrow to the hole in the wire. Wu Wang was of the opinion that even if they did block up the hole, the wombat would make another, and suggested that they should leave a heap of grass and any discarded or unsaleable vegetables just outside the hole. Bill would come upon the gifts and eat them and not trouble to enter the gardens.

Yet Yow and Hook Suey considered this to be a great plan, so at dusk that day they collected and laid out for Bill what they thought was a tempting repast—cabbage leaves, a few turnips which had run to seed, some spinach well past its prime and a heap of potato peelings.

When Bill emerged from his burrow some hours later, he pondered whether he should give the market garden a rest that night and seek a change of diet in the hills. The inner bark of a tree and perhaps a few roots might be nice for a change. And as he pondered the matter he ambled automatically down the track towards the gardens and, arriving at the hole in the fence, found it partially blocked with the Chinese offering.

The wombat narrowly inspected the heap of vegetation and thought precious little of it. Had he known that it was a gift from the Chinese, he would have felt insulted. A couple of cabbage leaves looked all right, so he ate them. The withered spinach and seeding turnips were, to him, so much garbage. So was the rest of the offering. He could see little profit in eating that rubbish when fresh-growing green vegetables lay just through the fence. So he stepped disdainfully over the stuff and entered the gardens.

By this time the moon had risen and her soft, silvery light showed up to perfection the choicest greens in the garden.

Bill, however, needed no heavenly light to illuminate his feast.

He was quietly enjoying himself in a bed of carrots close to the gardeners' hut when the door opened and into the moonlight stepped Wu Wang. He was carrying a billy can and intended to fill it with water from the tank at the side of the hut. This tank was only a few yards from the browsing wombat and Wu Wang, sighting Bill, gave an indignant grunt.

"Ungrateful and hideous pig, badger, beaver and wombat," he told Bill in Chinese. "You spurn our honourable offering of nice food and still steal from our gardens. Oh, you offspring of a thousand times ten thousand nameless and tailless dragons!"

Bill paused in his eating and, with a carrot top dangling from the corner of his mouth, raised his blunt head and looked Wu Wang over. His interest quickly fading, he swallowed the carrot top and then wrenched another from the earth, the carrot hanging on to it.

This proved a little too much for the indignant Wu Wang, who uttered a wild Chinese yell and hurled the billy can at Bill. The wombat stopped the can with his well-padded ribs and gave a startled snort, dropping his newly-won carrot as he did so. And when Wu Wang, following up the can, rushed madly at him and gave him a sound kick in the ribs, he decided that he was unwelcome in the gardens and made for the hole in the fence at a lumbering trot.

Wu Wang did not follow him. Retrieving the billy can, he filled it with water from the tank and returned to the hut to tell Hook Suey and Yet Yow that ingratitude was one of the leading traits of the Australian wombat. As for that ungrateful animal, it was heading for home, its feelings, and its ribs, more than a trifle sore. As Bill bedded down in his snug nest deep inside his burrow, he resolved mentally to strike the Chinese gardens off his list of visiting places. He was, he told himself, done for good with all human beings, especially Chinese.

But unfortunately for Bill the wombat, Chinese were not done for good with him. On the other side of the township, the lights of which in the far distance Bill had often inspected from the mouth of his burrow, a drama had been enacted that night—a drama in which the wombat was destined to take no small part.

CHAPTER FOUR

The Yellow Box

L ING YUANG paused as he bent down to raise the lid of the heavy iron box in the corner, gazed cautiously around with eyes in which the faintest gleam of suspicion shone for an instant, and sighed. There was nobody near. Slowly he raised the massive lid and stared pensively into the interior.

He was an old man. His spare frame had tottered as it moved across the room to the box and he had often felt lately that the sands of his life were running out. He desired nothing better than to be gathered quietly to the bosoms of his ancestors, and although his bones would not be allowed to mingle with the earth of his native land unless a miracle occurred—and Ling Yuang was no great believer in miracles—he was filled with a philosophical resignation.

The small Chinese quarter of the country town was not very picturesque. No flaming dragons gilded the doorways. No yards of gaudy brilliant cloth suggested the grandeur of the Orient that the old Chinese had known as a lad. In the street itself the yellow faces, peeping from under the brims of battered Occidental hats, and perhaps a certain naive gait, alone betrayed the East. Uninspiring Chinese writing over the doorways thick with dust and grime combined with the unlovely street itself to render it commonplace.

For several minutes Ling Yuang peered into the depths of the old iron box as if wrapped in thought, and then he slowly and reverently bent down and extracted a smaller box, the colour of gold, placed it on a nearby bamboo table and slowly closed the larger box.

The room itself was a decided contrast to the world outside and there was nothing in it to suggest that a few yards away ragged urchins played in the gutters and occasional traffic drifted up and down the dreary street. The room was typical of the unchanging Orient and was hidden by a thick curtain from the drab outlook. A bronze incense burner sent forth a thin stream of aromatic smoke in one corner, while carved screens of bamboo were so arranged as to hide the dinginess of the walls. If Ling Yuang had been attempting to transport a bit of old China to an unlovely part of Australia when he had arranged this room, he had but only partially succeeded.

There were certain yellow men in that street who would welcome the untimely death of this old Chinese for this might provide them with an opportunity to get their hands on his yellow box. Every Chinese living there, and quite a number of white men, too, knew of the existence of this box, but not one of them had ever tried to rob the old man of it. The Chinese were a little superstitious regarding it. Strange tales had been circulated about the box and, though certain nasty-minded white persons often dreamed of possessing it, up to date Ling Yuang had not been molested.

Ling Yuang was a bit of a mystery himself. He had no social dealings with the rest of his yellow brethren and they, as a whole, left him severely alone, visiting his small laundry only when necessity demanded it. Yet they all knew of this yellow box and there was hardly one of the slinking figures that crept nightly into Ah Foo's sinister doorway several yards up the street for an evening's gambling who would not cheerfully have slain several of his countrymen in order to wrap his fingers around it. Yet they did not molest Ling Yuang.

Ling Yuang was not a fool. He knew that the box was unsafe, yet he refused to hide it away. And he knew something else that not another soul on earth knew—that the contents of the yellow box were valueless to anyone except himself.

Picking up the box from the table, he slowly moved into the shop, placed it on the counter, closed the front door leading to the street, and locked it. The sun was already sinking and the urchins had gone home.

Hugging the yellow box closely, he passed out of the shop and entered a smaller room in the centre of which was a table with a deep red cushion on top. He placed the box on the centre of this cushion and stared at it sombrely. It was about six inches long, about the same width and four inches deep and bore a faint resemblance to a miniature cabin trunk.

Ling Yuang made no attempt to open the box, but continued his unwavering contemplation of it for a few minutes before moving off into a dark corner. Presently he came back carrying a small wooden tray on which reposed a saucer of boiled rice, a cup of some mysterious concoction and a jar of uncertain-looking liquid. These he arranged around the cushion and after a profound obeisance which nearly cracked his old bones, went softly out, closing the door behind him.

For many years, at precisely the same hour each day, Ling Yuang had gone through the same ritual. The small yellow box was taken from the large iron box, carried to the front

shop and placed on the counter while he closed and locked
the door, then taken to the other room and placed on the
cushion and finally surrounded by eatables, always fresh and
already prepared. There it remained until the morning, when
it was returned to its former receptacle, the large iron box.

When he returned to the other room, Ling Yuang sat
down on the large iron box and bowed his head on his chest
and waited—waited for the messenger who never came.

The running sands of thirty years had trickled through
the hour glass since the memorable day that the yellow box
had first become valuable to old Ling Yuang. One man alone
knew its history and that man was Ling Yuang. He thought
that two knew it, but the second had been gathered to his
ancestors long since. It was for the arrival of this friend that
Ling Yuang waited, unknowingly, in vain.

What his thoughts were as he sat huddled on the iron box
were entirely his own. Ling Yuang's secrets were unshared.
Did he, perhaps, dream of that memorable day in the far past
when the first and last great tragedy of his life had stalked
across the pathway of his soul and had rendered him even
more impassive than he would naturally have been, and
which had made the yellow box so infinitely precious to him?

Though the Chinese quarter did not know it, Ling Yuang
had had a son. Thirty years previously he had lost him. The
tiny child had perished in a fire which had destroyed the
hut in which Ling Yuang had lived with his friend Wong
Sue at the market garden they ran in partnership. Except
for the old clothes he had on at the time, Ling Yuang had
saved nothing, except the yellow box. Something else was
recovered from the fire debris some days later and now
reposed in that yellow box.

Ling Yuang's comrade in misfortune, the stolid Wong
Sue—the only other man who had known the secret of the

yellow box—was not so badly situated. He was a Chinese of some substance, whose final journey to the land of his fathers seemed assured. He had not believed in keeping all his worldly possessions in the old hut like Ling Yuang, and the fire was only a temporary setback to him. To Ling Yuang it was the cremation of years of labour and as he stared with dull eyes at the smouldering ruins that day, he knew that the fulfilment of his ambition was extremely remote. To add to his cup of bitterness, his cherished motherless son was put beyond the power of sending or taking his father's bones to China, or to any other place.

Ling Yuang and Wong Sue sold the market garden to three fellow countrymen—Hook Suey, Yet Yow and Wu Wang—and on his half of the proceeds, Wong Sue went off to Darwin to try his luck at pearling. Ling Yuang bought a small laundry in the Chinese quarter of the country town not very far away from the market gardens.

Through the years that followed, Ling Yuang, attending to an endless stream of shirts and collars, and barely making enough money to live in comfort, had infrequent news of Wong Sue's movements. There had been an understanding between them that when Wong Sue went back to China, the yellow box would go with him.

From Darwin, Wong Sue drifted down to Broome and there got himself mixed up in an argument with an evil white man over the price of a stolen pearl. The argument ended in the white man's favour. Wong Sue was laid to rest in the local cemetery but the white man was escorted to Perth and then to gaol.

But of this Ling Yuang knew absolutely nothing, so he still awaited the coming of his friend.

CHAPTER FIVE
The Theft of the Box

I<small>N</small> a dirty little room at the rear of Ah Foo's shop up the street, two heads were close together in deep discussion.

"Stiffen the crows, Bert," said Dan Hedge, a great hulking brute of a man with a broken nose and a dilapidated cloth cap, "I tell you the thing will be as easy as falling off a log. The old Pat will be on his pat and if he cuts up rusty, well, we'll dong him."

Bert McGinty, a little rat of a man, was not convinced.

"That's all right about that," he said, "but who'll do the dongin'?" Bert had a wholesome respect for his own skin and, though the object of their discussion was an old man, Bert was taking no chances.

Dan Hedge snorted in disgust.

"Come on up and keep yer mouth shut," he instructed. "If yer ain't game to come in with me and get yer share, yer can stay outside and keep nit."

Ling Yuang, apparently still deeply immersed in his contemplation of the infinite, did not hear them as they climbed through the window into the room where the cushion and its precious burden were. His old head remained sunk upon his scraggy chest.

"Dunno where it's likely to be," muttered Hedge as he and McGinty paused just inside the window. "Better get on with the searchin', Dan," muttered his companion uneasily. "I don't like this."

A few seconds later an excited whisper from Hedge brought McGinty to his side and together they stared down at the yellow box lying on the cushion. Hedge grabbed it excitedly and hugged it to his chest.

"May as well go through the place while we're here and see what we can pick up," he said. "The old Chow must be havin' a night out."

They crept silently into the little shop and got busy. In a few minutes everything portable and worth carting away, and it was not much, was stowed into two bags, the said bags being manufactured by the simple method of tying together the sleeves of a couple of shirts. The fact that two of Ling Yuang's customers were going to take a mighty poor view of the use to which their garments were being put, did not disturb the two intruders.

Closely followed by McGinty, Hedge passed into the room where the old Chinese was huddled up on the iron box. They saw him and paused uncertainly.

"Don't wake 'im up for Pete's sake," implored McGinty in a whisper. "Let's get out of 'ere as quick as we can while it's safe."

"Hold this and shut up," hissed Hedge as he thrust the yellow box into McGinty's hands. McGinty was already encumbered with two shirts filled with stolen articles, but he managed to keep hold of the box.

Hedge crept silently towards the Chinese. Between him and the old man lay an ancient rug and as he stepped on to it, McGinty sneaked forward and grabbed him by the shoulder, meaning to restrain him in whatever he intended to do. The action caused Hedge to jump. The rug slipped from under his feet and he fell, colliding heavily with Ling Yuang who, under the force of the impact, fell sideways to the floor and remained still.

"You've done for 'im!" whined McGinty in terror.

"How could a little bump like that 'urt anyone?" asked Hedge wonderingly.

"Well, don't stand there gogglin' at 'im. Let's get out of 'ere!" howled the panic-stricken McGinty. He laid hands on the man whom all his life he had been afraid of, and literally dragged him to the open window. In a few seconds they were outside and racing up the dirty back lane, Hedge clasping the yellow box. In the excitement the shirt-bags had been left behind. They did not return to Ah Foo's shop but, after a short consultation, made their way by devious paths out of the town and into the bush, arriving finally at a lonely old deserted humpy that they sometimes used as a rendezvous.

This old hut once had been occupied by an eccentric character named Ben Grant, an old-age pensioner, but Ben had been dead for some time now. He had fallen into a nearby quarry one night while on a spree, and had broken his neck. The hut was a lonely place and was shunned by most folk because it had the reputation of being haunted.

Closing the door and noting that the broken window was covered by a corn bag, Hedge ventured to strike a match and to light a stump of candle which stood in an empty bottle on a ricketty table. Cold beads of perspiration stood on McGinty's forehead, but Hedge was cooler now that he was safely away from old Ling Yuang's shop. He placed the yellow box on the table and looked at it avidly.

"Wonder what's in it?" he said. "Can't be much after all, because it ain't a very big box. Maybe it is full of sovereigns.

They'd be worth a lot of dough these days."

"'I don't think it's heavy enough," said McGinty. "Anyway, 'ow are yer gonna open the thing? The lid is a very tight fit and there's only a very little 'ole to git a key in. An' we ain't got no key."

Hedge searched around the hut for some sort of tool to use on the box, but found nothing. He took a small penknife from his pocket and tried to find a crevice in which to insert the blade, but there was none. He then made a jab at the keyhole with the knife and broke the point off it.

He was staring sullenly at the yellow box when he gave a sudden start and McGinty let out a sharp yelp. Something had thudded on the roof of the hut.

"What the heck was that, Dan?" exclaimed McGinty in terror.

"I dunno, but I'm gonna try to find out," said Hedge. "Just a minute."

He blew out the candle and sneaked to the door, opening it slowly. As he did so, there was another thud, as if somebody were throwing stones on the roof. He opened the door and stared into the night for a few seconds but, seeing nothing, closed it again and relit the candle.

"I don't like this, Bert," he said. "I think we'd better clear out of here. We'll hide the box and do a get. Nobody comes near this place. You can tell by the length of the candle that no one 'as been 'ere since we was 'ere ourselves and that must be a coupla weeks ago. I'll dig a 'ole in the floor under the table and bury the box for safety and we'll come back later. It's safer than 'avin' the thing on us."

McGinty agreed. Hedge quickly scraped a hole in the earthen floor, dropped the box into it and covered it up. The two of them waited a few minutes expecting to hear more thuds on the roof, but these did not eventuate. Hedge blew out the candle and he and McGinty left the hut as furtively as they had arrived and made their way back to the township. They parted on a corner, Hedge stating that he was going straight home to bed. McGinty mentioned that he would spend an hour or so at Ah Foo's before he sought his bunk.

Bert McGinty was a dishonest man, even with his own friends. He did go to Ah Foo's shop, but his stay there was brief. From the Chinese he borrowed certain articles and then he made his way by a long and circuitous route back to the hut in the bush and the yellow box.

Nearing the former residence of the late Mr. Grant, McGinty became ultra-cautious. He remembered the mysterious thumps on the roof—the thumps that had caused Hedge to bury the box and bolt. McGinty was very cowardly by nature, but the thought of the rich treasures the yellow box might contain, overcame his natural timidity.

"It was probably nothing but a 'possum," he muttered to himself as he crept round the corner of the hut. "Them things come around 'ouses and sheds and even build their nests in the roofs. Yes, I'll bet it was just an old 'possum chasin' its mate or something."

Having thus reassured himself, the little man crept up to the door and, after a quick look round at the silent bush, sidled inside and quickly shut the door.

Now, had Hedge and McGinty known just what had caused those mysterious bumps on the roof, they might not have left the box behind in the hut. McGinty, the timid, would not have had the courage to return. He and Hedge had been quite confident that their presence in the hut was unknown to anybody But somebody knew that somebody had been at the hut.

The mysterious thumps on the roof had been caused by

two small boys, Herbert Long and Clarence Doolan. Out for nocturnal adventures so dear to the heart of the venture-some young Australian, they had been passing the "haunted hut" and, in sheer bravado, had challenged each other to fire stones from their catapults on to the roof to demonstrate their unbelief in ghosts and all such non-existent rubbish.

But when Hedge had opened the door and they had glimpsed the shadowy figure of a man, their professed un-belief had turned into stunned conviction; and as soon as the door had closed again, they had bolted as fast as they could for home and mother, certain that they had seen the ghost of the late lamented Mr. Grant.

McGinty, blissfully unaware of all this, did not light the candle when he entered the hut. He knew every inch of the interior and quickly unearthed the yellow box from the spot under the table. He refilled the hole and within seconds was out of the hut and into the shelter of the bush.

The little man did not return at once to the township. He had his plans. He was going to hide the yellow box again and then leave town for a time until things had blown over and his friend Hedge had had time to calm down. He was not wise enough to realise that his very absence might make his friend highly suspicious when he found out that the box was missing.

Reaching a small clearing in the bush, McGinty untied the bundle he had brought from Ah Foo's. First of all he spread out a small waterproof sheet. On this he placed the yellow box and on top of the box laid a piece of flat lead. Then he wrapped box and lead up in the sheeting, securing the parcel with stout wire. To this he attached a length of rope.

Passing through the bush he made his way to the bottom of the quarry into which Ben Grant had fallen with such fatal results, and came to a halt at the edge of a waterhole.

After carefully examining his surroundings and memorising certain geographical details, he quietly dropped the box into the water which, at that spot, was several feet deep, holding on to the end of the rope as he did so. The free end of the rope he laid in the mud and over it he arranged some stones.

It was not until he had walked around the hole a couple of times and subjected the whole layout to a very careful scrutiny, that he was completely satisfied. Then, with a soft chuckle of contentment, he made his way quietly homewards.

CHAPTER SIX

Bill Becomes a Ghost

SERGEANT MURPHY was in his room at the police station when a constable poked his head around the door and told him that a friend of his wanted an interview.

"But I have so many friends, Constable Osborne. That is the penalty for being so popular," said Murphy. "Which one is this—the Governor General or the Prime Minister?"

"I can't remember Chows being elected to those high positions," said Osborne with a grin. "So it can't be either."

"A Chow?" asked the surprised Sergeant. "I didn't know I had any friends among the Chinese. I know most of them, but I can't say that they are friends of mine. For some reason they seem to object to my asking them questions about gambling and smoking opium and so on. Which one is this?"

"Old Ling Yuang, the bloke who runs the laundry," said Osborne.

"Can't be," said the sergeant. "Old Ling Yuang never leaves his shirts and collars or that mysterious yellow box everyone knows he has."

"Well, he's left them all this morning, anyway," said the constable.

"Okay. Shoot him in and I'll see what he has on his

conscience," said Murphy briskly.

Osborne withdrew with a nod and presently old Ling Yuang shuffled into Murphy's presence, to be greeted with a cheery "And how are the shirts this morning, John?"

Ling Yuang stared gravely at the sergeant for a few seconds and then, in precise English, said, "Mister Murphy, I have been robbed. Last night some persons came to my shop and stole my yellow box."

Murphy gave a low whistle and his eyes filled with interest. So it had happened at last!

"Tell me about it." he invited, and the old Chinese told him all he knew—which was not a great deal. He had been dozing in his shop when suddenly he had been knocked over by somebody. By the time he had recovered himself the intruders had gone, taking with them his yellow box.

"You must find it for me, Mister Murphy," he said. "It is the most honourable and precious thing that I own. I would rather give up my life than that box."

"Why is it?" asked the sergeant. "What does it contain that makes it so precious?"

"That does not matter," responded Ling Yuang. "The box has not been opened for many years and there is nobody who can open it but myself. What it contains is my own business."

"I don't know so much about that," said Murphy. "I've got to know what I am looking for, you know."

"I shall describe the box to you," said the old Chinese, and did so, in great detail.

"And what did you say was inside it?" asked the sergeant.

"I did not say and I am not going to say," said Ling Yuang and, without another word, left the room.

"Hey, wait a minute," exclaimed Murphy, heaving himself from his chair and following Ling Yuang into the street.

Catching him up, he told him that he would visit the shop and examine it to see if he could find any clues. Ling Yu-ang nodded in silent agreement, and together they made their way to the shop. It was a long walk and during the trip, Murphy asked the old man if he had any idea who the thieves might have been. Ling Yuang could not help him on that. He merely mentioned that it could have been any one of a dozen persons, white or yellow.

The examination of the shop did not help the sergeant in the least, and after a few inquiries un and down the street, which yielded him no information, he decided to pay a visit to the Chinese gardens to question Hook Suey, Yet Yow and Wu Wang.

When he got there, the only person he could see was Hook Suey, who was carefully extracting weeds from be-tween a row of cabbages.

"Fine lot of cabbages you have there, John," Murphy remarked and Hook Suey immediately tried to sell him one. Murphy waved the vegetable aside and got down to business.

"I'm from the police," he said unnecessarily.

"Ai. I know you, Missa Murphy. Whaffor you come here?" said Hook Suey uneasily.

"To admire your spuds," said the sergeant. "One Murphy among the others, if you grasp my point."

"No savvy," blinked Hook Suey.

"Skip it," said Murphy. "Now listen, Charlie Chan, tell me all your darkest secrets. Do you know a Chinese named Ling Yuang?"

"Not know that feller," said Hook Suey promptly.

"Now that's a lie to start with," said the sergeant. "Didn't you and your cobbers buy this garden from him and another Chinese years and years ago?"

"Ai," agreed Hook Suey, "but not know him now."

"I see," said Murphy, who did not see at all. "Ever heard about a yellow box he owns?"

"Know about box. Him Ling Yuang have yellow box. Everyone know," said Hook Suey.

"What is in the thing?"

"Not know."

"Plenty of money, huh?"

"Mebbe. Not know."

"I bet you'd like to get your hands on it, John!"

Hook Suey's face crinkled into a rare smile.

"Ai," he agreed. "Muchee good. But no chance. Him Ling Yuang, him look after box muchee welly careful."

"By the way," said Murphy, "where are your two mates? Are they at home?"

"Wu Wang and Yet Yow, him go after ghost," said Hook Suey gravely

"Go after what?" ejaculated the sergeant in astonishment. "Ghost?"

"Ai," nodded Hook Suey. "Him pig ghost walk about on lettucee all night. No good ghost walkee on lettucee. Kill 'um quick."

Murphy looked closely at the Chinese, suspecting him of some sort of obscure Oriental joke, but there was nothing humorous about Hook Suey.

"Me see 'um plentee time," he resumed. "Him walkee out of hills, tread on lettucee, cabbagee, eat 'um carrot. No good. Me good feller, but no likee ghost on vegetable. Him bad feller him pig ghost. No good."

"You're as mad as a snake," said Murphy insultingly.

"Not mad. See 'um pig ghost."

"Pig ghost? Pig?" The sergeant broke off suddenly. Light dawned on him. "You wouldn't be talking about your pet wombat, would you?"

"Ai," grunted the Chinese. "Lombat. No good. Kill 'um cabbagee."

"Yes, but the thing is not a ghost," protested Murphy. "What is all this in aid of?"

Slowly and carefully Hook Suey explained what he meant. He told Murphy all about the wombat's visits, including the episode of the billy can. Since that night Bill had acted like a ghost. Sometimes the gardeners saw him, but at other times they did not: Bill seemed able to make himself invisible, but he still raided the vegetables.

Murphy was not very interested in wombats and said so. Asked where Yet Yow and Wu Wang were, Hook Suey said that his friends had gone off into the hills to see if they could locate the wombat's burrow and deal with its occupant.

"I wish them joy," said the sergeant, and made his way back to the police station.

Several days passed without incident. There was no news of the missing box. Then Murphy decided to pay another visit to the Chinese gardens. He could not get it out of his head that the three Chinese were not completely innocent of complicity in the theft. Why he had that idea he did not know, but he had it.

Arriving at the gardens, he found that once again Hook Suey was the only one at home. That placid yellow man told him that Yet Yow and Wu Wang were away.

"Chase 'um lombat," he explained.

"What again?" snorted Murphy. "Every time I come here, your mates are out chasing wombats. Didn't they do any good last time?"

"Find lombat hole, but velly deep," said Hook Suey.

"What are they going to do now?"

"Make fire, smoke him out," said the Chinese. "Then hunt him right away. No good lombat tread on cabbagee.

Him pig ghost."

"I think you are three ratbags," exclaimed Murphy. "Goodbye." Saying which, he returned to the police station. There a surprise was in store for him.

Impatiently awaiting his arrival were two small boys who had an interesting story to tell. In common with every resident of the small town, the lads knew all about Ling Yuang's mysterious box and that it had been stolen.

Well, they had found the box—and had lost it again!

CHAPTER SEVEN

The Boy in the Burrow

THE two lads were greatly excited and also were filled with a sense of their own importance. They insisted on bellowing together into Murphy's ear. The sergeant stood it for exactly three seconds and then adopted stern measures.

"Shut up!" he roared. They shut up as if their eloquence had been turned off like a tap.

"Here, you," said Murphy, singling out the elder of the two, a very thin and tall youngster of about 11 years of age, with a face liberally spattered with freckles. "You tell me the yarn and remember, I want the truth, the whole truth and nothing but the truth. See?"

The boy nodded but became tongue-tied all of a sudden. "Well, come on, Skinny, get it off your chest," the sergeant invited patiently.

"Don't call me Skinny. I don't like it," grunted the lad. "Anyway, Clarence here can tell you better than I can."

His mate Clarence, who was slightly chubby and had a shock of sandy-coloured hair, favoured him with a rather baleful stare, but resolutely remained silent.

"Listen, we're not here all day," said Murphy. "Speak up."

"Herbert hooked the dashed thing out of the mudhole.

He can tell you," said Clarence, breaking his silence.

"I won't," said Herbert, who, for once, was a boy of few words. Murphy glanced from one to the other and they returned the glance with interest but in stubborn silence.

"Look here, you two," snorted the impatient sergeant. "What the heck is the matter with you? A moment ago I couldn't shut you up. Get a move on, will you? Now then you, Skinny, or Herbert, or whatever your name is, tee up and drive off."

"Don't call me Skinny!" roared Herbert. "Drive off where?"

"Oh, skip it. Apparently you have never done any golf caddying. Get on with the yarn," said the weary Murphy.

"Very well then," said Herbert with dignity. "I shall tell you what went on. It was this way…"

His shyness vanishing, the lad launched into his story. His mate Clarence was disposed at times to interrupt him with marginal notes, but Murphy quickly put a stop to that.

"Me and Clarence," stated Herbert, "was out after blackberries this morning but we didn't have no luck. Dunno why."

"Push on," said Murphy. "The mere fact that this is the wrong season for blackberries probably was overlooked by you. Mind you, I advance that reason purely as my own personal opinion and will not be in the least offended if you decide not to accept it."

"The bush," declared Clarence simply, "was as free from blackberries as a frog is from feathers."

"Naturally," said Murphy. "The wrong time of the year, as I told you. I don't know what has come over the kids these days. When I was a youngster in the bush we knew all the seasons—when the blackberries were out, the months all the birds nested, and so forth and so on."

"You must have been a very clever kid," sneered Clarence.

"I suppose that is why they made you a sergeant."

"Less of the insults," said Murphy. "Stick to the black berries."

"We didn't get none," said Herbert. "So we decided to have a stickybeak at the old quarry what old Ben Grant fell into and busted his neck."

"How do you know it was the same quarry?" asked Murphy, who had, months previously, investigated the death of old Ben Grant.

"There ain't much goes on in these parts that we don't know about. We get around," replied Herbert proudly.

"Don't kid yourself," said Murphy.

"You bet your life we do," broke in Clarence, who was determined to take some part in the debate. "And what is more, mister, he still haunts it, too. My word he does. It would give me the ginger willies to go there at night-time."

"Who haunts what?" demanded the sergeant.

"Old Ben Grant haunts the quarry, him being dead and becoming a dirty big ghost," explained Clarence earnestly. "I seen him myself at the quarry, not so long ago, neither."

"When was it, exactly?" asked the sergeant, interested in spite of his desire to learn about the yellow box.

"One night about a week ago," said Clarnce.

"A minute ago you said you would never go near the quarry at night for fear you would contract a severe dose of the ginger willies," Murphy pointed out.

"Take no notice of Clarence, mister," said Herbert. "He's an awful young liar. He knows it was not at the quarry at all, but at his old hut in the bush."

"How long have you owned an old hut in the bush, Clarrie?" Murphy inquired.

"Old Ben's hut," said Herbert with a touch of irritation. Clarence turned a baleful, yet warning eye upon his mate and then instructed him to shut his face and to keep it shut.

"We ain't at no time," he said, slowly and carefully selecting his words, "been near any dashed hut in no dashed bush and you dashed well know it, Herbert."

"Oh, so you two saw a ghost at old Grant's humpy in the bush, did you?" asked Murphy. And as Clarence and Herbert began to shuffle their feet about, he added, "I guess you were up to no good hanging around that hut. No doubt you were there to see what you could steal, but we won't go into that for the moment. Get on with the yarn about the quarry and the blackberries. We will leave the haunting until later."

It was Clarence who took up the story. He said that he and Herbert had gone to the quarry to see if they could catch yabbies in the waterhole. They noticed the box in the water, fished it out and tried to open it. Not succeeding, they decided to take it to the police station.

"I suppose that if you had managed to open it and had found something worth stealing in it, the police would never have heard from you," said Murphy cynically.

"We ain't all like the coppers," said Clarence cuttingly.

"What do you mean by that remark?" inquired the sergeant, smiling to himself.

"Work it out for yourself," replied Clarence frigidly. "Anyway, that box wasn't in the waterhole the day before because we was both there looking for some cows and didn't see it."

"What were the cows doing in the waterhole?" demanded Murphy.

Clarence sighed wearily. Murphy was getting under his skin. Clarence was a lad who did not enjoy having his leg pulled.

"The cows," he said heavily, "wasn't in the waterhole.

They was feeding nearby. Me and Herbert went down to the waterhole and filled in a bit of time firing rocks at an old kerosene tin with our gongeyes."

"Correct," said Herbert briefly.

"And what, may I ask, is a gongeye?" asked the sergeant with interest. Clarence and Herbert looked at him with raised eyebrows. Clarence's lip curled slightly, while Herbert sneered faintly.

"What sort of a policeman was this?" wondered Clarence. As a reader of bloodthirsty literature which detailed the adventures of Dead Shot Dan and Coyote Claude and other persons of a similar kidney, who appeared to spend a remarkable existence committing daily murders in western American mining camps, shooting up sheriffs and holding up stage coaches, Clarence had little use for law and order. He had learned long since that sheriffs, troopers and other types of policemen were just stupid fools. That being so, he felt it incumbent upon him to explain clearly to this mutton-headed mug Murphy.

"A gongeye," he said, "is a catapult or, if you like, a sling-shot." He paused and sneered. "You make them out of a hunk of elastic and a forked stick with a leather pouch to hold the rocks."

"Oh, you mean a shanghai!" nodded Murphy. "That is what we used to call them as kids."

"What did you call 'em when they was grown-ups?" grunted Herbert.

"Get on with the ghost yarn," retorted the sergeant.

Neither Clarence nor Herbert seemed inclined to discuss it, but the sergeant managed to overcome their reluctance by throwing out sinister threats of imprisonment. They then took it in turns to relate the story. They told him that they had been out for a walk in the bush and as they were passing the old hut, saw a light in it.

"What were you doing in the bush at that hour of the night?" asked Murphy accusingly.

"At what hour?" asked Clarence coldly. "We never said no particular hour. The way you talk you'd think it was midnight. Well, it wasn't."

"The point is well taken," admitted Murphy with a grin. "I'll change the question by asking you what you were doing in the bush at all at night."

Clarence and Herbert looked at him askance. It was just like a copper to ask inconvenient questions. They had got nothing out of the Chinese gardens, anyway. The melons wouldn't be ripe yet for weeks. Murphy noted their uneasiness and chuckled to himself. He did not repeat the question.

"Don't get conscience-stricken," he said. "Just box on with the main story."

Clarence told him that as soon as they saw the light in the hut they made a combined dive for the safety of some bushes. Reaching these, they paused and looked fearfully at the old humpy.

"Herbert bet me I wasn't game to fire a road apple on to the roof out of me gongeye and I said I was game if he was, so we fired a couple of road apples, one each," he said.

"May I inquire exactly what a road apple is?"

"Ah, gee!" snorted Clarence disgustedly. "A brick, a stone, a gibber, a rock!"

"Ha!" said the sergeant. "Well, get on with it." Herbert looked at him impressively.

"As true as I'm standing here, Mr. Murphy, old Ben Grant come to the door and looked at me, right in the eye-clean in the eyeball," he said in awe-stricken tones. "Yessir, clean in the eyeball."

"Stiffen the nanny goats," said Clarence, not to be outdone, "he looked me right clean between the two eyeballs. My word he did!"

"Upon which," commented the cynical Murphy, "you both turned and bolted like the merry dickens."

Clarence and Herbert glared at him reproachfully.

"What would you have done?" demanded Clarence bitterly. "Rushed up and donged him over the head with a rock?"

"I know what he would have done, Clarence," said Herbert, who felt very keenly the implied slur on their courage. "He would have run like mad, too."

"You have not answered my question," persisted the sergeant. "Did you, or did you not, run like the merry dickens?"

"We did, and faster than that, too," chorused the two lads with simple dignity. Then something appeared to amuse Clarence. He chuckled.

"You couldn't see Herbert's hoofs for dust and small gibbers," he grinned reminiscently.

"That so? I did hear that they are gonna send you to the next Olympic Games," Herbert told him cuttingly.

"What makes you think it was old Ben Grant you saw?" asked Murphy, repressing a laugh. "He is dead, you know. It might have been any man. You were a fair distance away, I gather."

"It was old Ben, and no error," said Herbert definitely.

"Are you quite certain it wasn't a wombat?"

"A what?" howled Clarence.

"A wombat. Don't you know what a wombat is?"

"Of course I know what a wombat is. Think I came down in the last shower?" grunted Clarence. "No, it was not a wombat."

"Very well then. Now we come to the most important point. Where the dickens is the box?"

"Lost," said Herbert dolefully.

"Yes, but how, where and when?"

"Well, now," said Herbert, "it happened this way. We couldn't open the thing so we decided to bring it along to the police station. But not straight away. We was going to look for birds' nests and didn't want to be bothered lugging it around with us, so we just shoved it down a big hole in the side of the hill and put a few broken branches and things over the entrance to hide it. When we came back a couple of hours afterwards, it had vamoosed."

"You two jokers are not having me on, are you?" asked the sergeant suspiciously.

"No fear," said Clarence. "You come with us to the hole and we'll show you where we left the box."

"All right," said Murphy briskly. "Let's go."

He led the way from the police station, Clarence and Herbert bringing up the rear. They got into a police car outside and Murphy drove off towards the quarry. They left the car at the closest point they could reach and after climbing through a fence and crossing a paddock, reached the quarry and the waterhole it contained. Herbert and Clarence pointed out the spot where they had found the wrapped-up box and then, with Herbert in the lead, they climbed out of the quarry and eventually reached the hillside overlooking the Chinese gardens, where Bill the wombat had his residence. Herbert pointed out the large hole in the side of the hill and at twigs and branches scattered about.

"We left this here hole covered up," he said. "While we was away after the birds' nests, somebody came here and removed the bushes and pinched the box out of the hole."

Sergeant Murphy did not answer. His keen eyes were taking in all the details. He noted the well-worn hole with its arched entrance and the faintly discernible track leading down the hillside. Other tell-tale signs confirmed his unspoken opinion that this was not just any old hole in the ground. Murphy was a good bushman.

"Do you two kids know what sort of a hole this is?" he asked. The two lads shook their heads.

"It's a wombat's burrow," said Murphy.

"Hey?" exclaimed Herbert. "Wombat? You don't mean to say that a dirty big wombat lives in this hole and has pinched the box?"

"No, I do not. Wombats rarely come out in daylight. I'll bet that human beings have removed the box. How far in did you push it?"

"Only about a couple of feet," said Clarence. "Maybe a horse or a cow came along and pulled the branches and twigs away," said Herbert brightly.

"And how could a horse or a cow get the box out?" asked his friend.

"Perhaps the box is right down the hole. How about crawling in and finding out?" asked Murphy. "The wombat may have come out for a breath of fresh air and knocked down the twigs covering the entrance. Then, on his way back in, he might have pushed the box right in."

"And pigs might fly," said Clarence with a sneer. "Anyway, I'm not small enough to crawl down that hole. Hang it, it might go right into the hillside for two miles."

"Your mate could make it," suggested Murphy. "He's long and thin."

"Oh, is he?" snorted Herbert. "Well, he ain't gonna try."

"Go on, Herbert, give it a fly," invited Clarence. "You could crawl into that hole. No need to go right down to the end."

"Yes, give it a go, Skinny," encouraged Murphy.

"Listen, don't keep calling me Skinny!" roared Herbert

violently. He paused and brooded intensely for a few moments.

"Will you kindly inform me," he said in icy tones, "how I shall get out of that hole if I am stuck in it? Will you kindly let me know what I shall do if I shall meet the wombat when I am stuck tight in the hole? Do you think I am as silly as I look?"

"You couldn't be," said the sergeant.

"Thank you very much," replied Herbert with cold dignity.

"That hole is quite big enough for you to crawl into," said Murphy. "Do you think I'd ask you to do it if I thought harm would come to you?"

"I wouldn't put anything past you," said Herbert grimly.

"Look here, all you have to do is to crawl in a couple of feet," said the sergeant. "We'll drag you out if you can't get out under your own steam. As for the wombat, I don't think it will be inside. As a matter of fact, this looks like an old burrow to me. Probably has not been used for years and years."

"And maybe it is now full of snakes, and death adders and dirty big trapdoor spiders," said Herbert.

"I'll give you five bob if you'll give it a fly," said Murphy.

"Cough it up," said Herbert promptly.

"Not so fast," said the sergeant. "Two bob now and three bob when you come out."

"Box or no box?"

"Box or no box," agreed the sergeant, tossing Herbert a florin which the lad deftly caught in mid-air. Dropping down on to the ground he flattened himself out and began to crawl into the burrow. He wriggled along until only his bare feet were protruding. In muffled tones he announced that he could see nothing and feel nothing.

"I'll go a bit further in," he said, and before either Clarence or the sergeant could comment, his feet had disappeared from view. Murphy got down on his knees and peered into the burrow. He could just see the soles of a pair of feet wriggle before vanishing into the darkness.

"Hope he doesn't get stuck," he murmured. "The silly young goat should not have gone in so far. It will be lovely if he gets stuck and we have to dig him out with shovels!"

CHAPTER EIGHT

Not Nice For Bill

B ILL the wombat, in all innocence, was sleeping peacefully in his nest at the end of his burrow, curled up as much as his bulk would permit. Suddenly he was wide awake. It was just like that. One moment, fast asleep dreaming of extra-special cabbages and lettuces, next moment, alert and wary. What had awakened him he did not know—yet. It was not time for him to set out on his nightly ramble, because he had only been bedded down for a few hours.

Something was going on that was not quite according to the rules. Bill lay awake without moving a hair, his ears strained to catch the slightest sound. And then he became uneasily aware of the fact that he was not alone in his burrow. Something had entered, and though it was still near the entrance, it was in the burrow all right.

This, Bill told himself, called for immediate investigation, so he heaved himself to his feet, pointed his nose towards daylight, and began to shuffle in that direction. The burrow, from the outside world to the nest chamber, was all of eighteen feet long, but the nest itself was round a corner from the straight tunnel. Bill had to go five feet before he reached the turn and when he did, he shoved his nose around the corner and sniffed.

In ordinary circumstances, provided the burrow was clear, he would have glimpsed a circle of light. But these were not ordinary circumstances and the burrow was not clear. Bill saw a gleam of light, but it was a curious wavering thin flicker as if something were rising and falling like a ship on a slight swell at sea—or as if some great creature were heaving and undulating in the tunnel, now allowing some of the outside light to become visible, now shutting it off altogether.

And that is what it was. The phenomenon was being caused by the heaving body of Herbert as he crawled slowly and painfully along the burrow. He was making a very tedious progress, literally dragging himself along by his hands because there was very little clearance. When Bill sighted him he had gone no distance at all, the soles of his feet being still within a yard of the burrow mouth.

Bill rounded the corner and as his eyes were accustomed to seeing in dark places, he readily perceived that he was not alone. But he could not quite make out what his mysterious visitor might be. Bill was no coward, so he decided to make a closer investigation. With his nose as straight out as nature would permit, he made towards the intruder, and as he neared Herbert, that lad gave a sudden heave forward to receive Bill's nose clean in the right eye.

The howl of pain and terror that echoed down the tunnel made Bill recoil on his haunches, and when something clawed wildly at him and then punched him violently, he turned tail and fled back to his nest, there to lie in palpitating terror while the unfortunate Herbert, who had done the clawing and punching while trying to get at his eye with his hand to rub it, began to back out of the burrow as best he could, roaring and bellowing loudly as he did so.

If it had been difficult for him to enter the tunnel, it was far harder to get out. He crayfished backwards an inch or two at a time, and probably would have taken a very long time to reach fresh air had not Sergeant Murphy, who was anxiously peering into the hole, sighted his feet and, grabbing them, literally dragged him out.

Herbert was a very distressed-looking lad when he rose to his feet, one hand rubbing his right eye furiously. His clothes were caked with dirt and tears of self-pity dropped from his left eye to make miniature drains through the dirt on his cheek.

"What was all the yelling and cursing in aid of?" demanded Murphy.

"I've been attacked and assaulted," sobbed Herbert. "Something sneaked up on me in that dashed hole and punched me in the eye. It must have been that old wombat, or a dingo or something. I was just crawling in when it rushed at me and hit me in the eye."

"What with?" asked Clarence curiously.

"How do I know what with?" yelled Herbert. "With his fist, I suppose. Do you think I stayed in there to ask him, you fool? Anyway, he hit me in the eye and if it turns black, who is gonna believe me when I tell them that a wombat clouted me?"

"That's your lookout," said Murphy callously. "Why the heck didn't you punch it back?"

"You ever had a fight with a wombat down a dirty big hole? You ever been clouted in the eye by a wombat?" asked Herbert bitterly. "Anyway, I did clout him back and he went for the lick of his life. Now, gimme the other three bob. I'm going home. I've had this business."

"What about the yellow box?" asked the sergeant.

"There ain't no box in that hole, yellow, pink, blue or

brindle. It's gone," said Herbert mournfully. "I'm going home. Hooray."

"If we'd found the thing we could have put it back in the waterhole where you found it and then set a watch on it to catch the person who put it there," grunted Murphy. "Now it's lost again."

A sudden thought struck him. Earlier in the day, when he had interviewed Hook Suey, that yellow person had told him that his two friends, Wu Wang and Yet Yow, had, that morning, gone out to smoke the wombat from his burrow. Now, supposing they had found the burrow blocked up, had removed the branches and twigs, discovered the box, realised what it was, and taken it back to the gardens?

"Come on, you two," he said tersely to Herbert and Clarence. "I think I know who got the yellow box and if I find it I want you to identify it."

Saying which, the sergeant left the wombat's burrow and climbed down the slope, followed obediently by Clarence and Herbert, the latter still rubbing his eye and muttering to himself dark things about silly policemen and murderous wombats.

Murphy crawled through the hole in the wire netting made by Bill the wombat, and the two lads crawled in after him. The sergeant was heading for the humpy home of the Chinese when he caught sight of Hook Suey fussing around some beehives in a secluded corner of the gardens. There were nine hives and the Chinese appeared to be depriving them of their honey stocks. He had a bit of mosquito net tied around his head and he was squirting smoke into the open top of a hive with a small pair of bellows. Approaching warily, Murphy hailed him from a safe distance.

"Come over here, John, I want you," he shouted. Obediently, Hook Suey suspended operations on the hive and joined him.

"Where are your two mates, Wu Wang and Yet Yow?" asked Murphy.

"No savvy," replied Hook Suey.

"Do you mean that you don't know where they are, or that you don't understand the question?" asked the sergeant impatiently. "I've got no time to be working out Chinese jigsaw puzzles."

"Not know," said the Chinese. "Wu Wang, Yet Yow, go town."

"Well, did they trap that wombat, or smoke him out, or whatever it was you told me this morning they intended doing?"

"No smoke out lombat. Forget to takee matches," said Hook Suey blandly.

"Yeah? Like a bloke going out to take pictures and leaving his camera at home. Don't give me that!"

"No trap lombat," said Hook Suey.

"What was it they found in the wombat's burrow that made them hurry home so fast?" asked Murphy, making a shot in the dark.

"No savvy," said the Chinese.

"All right, then, don't savvy," snorted Murphy. "I hope your useless bees sting you to death. Come on, you two," he added, turning to Herbert, who had developed a wonderful black eye, and Clarence. "Let us go to town and see if we can find those other Chows. A man may as well talk to a post as to this bee-robbing coot."

Murphy and his two young companions searched all likely haunts in town but could not find the missing Wu Wang and Yet Yow. He was certain now that they had found the yellow box in the wombat's tunnel, and he was determined to find them. But he did not succeed and some hours later he confided his suspicions to Constable Osborne.

"I'm going to visit their place tonight and give them a shock," he said darkly.

"If they did get the box from the wombat, they will have got rid of it before then," objected the constable.

"I'll find out what they have done with it if I have to knock their yellow heads together," replied the sergeant with a confidence he was far from feeling.

CHAPTER NINE

Not Nice For Murphy

JUST on dusk, Sergeant Murphy and Constable Osborne paid a visit to the Chinese gardens and found only Hook Suey in residence, as they had half-expected. Hook Suey told them that he had no idea where Yet Yow and Wu Wang were, but added that no doubt they would turn up in due course.

"Well, I can't hang around waiting for them to come home," said Murphy. "I'm going to the pictures tonight. Come on, Osborne."

The two police officers departed, but they did not go to the pictures. When darkness was complete, they returned furtively to the gardens and hid themselves in a spot from which they could observe any arrivals or departures from the Chinese humpy. They selected a deep ditch on one side of the property. This was completely dry, but was carpeted with thick couch grass. Between them and the fence was a small shrub which effectually concealed them from view.

It was a coincidence that at the precise moment that Murphy and Osborne were making themselves comfortable in the ditch, Bill the wombat, leaving his nest and arriving at the entrance to his burrow, poked his head outside and tested the air with his nose.

The wombat was not feeling his best and brightest. Physically he was in fair shape, but spiritually he was uneasy and upset. The encounter with the mysterious visitor that morning was still very fresh in his mind. He did not like it one little bit. The whole security of his home had been challenged. How did he know that such a thing would not occur again? It was more than a trifle disconcerting to any wombat to realise that at any hour of the day or night his domain might be invaded by mysterious monsters that clawed at him and punched his nose. He was not afraid of ordinary enemies that he could see; he was as courageous as the next wombat, come to that; but he did ask that antagonists show themselves and not go crawling into his burrow in such a manner that he could make neither head nor tail of them.

His inspection of the outside worlds satisfied him that no immediate danger was to be apprehended, so he trotted off down the slope towards the flat where, for a time, he feasted on grass and a few roots which he gouged out of the ground. Then he made his way to the Chinese gardens, crawled through the hole in the wire netting and commenced to forage around.

Murphy and Osborne in their ditch did not see Bill and he was unaware of their presence in the immediate neighborhood.

That there was somebody at home in the humpy was evident by the partly-opened door, out of which shone a dim light. In actual fact, Hook Suey was there and, by the light of a lone candle, was engaged in the interesting task of separating honey from beeswax. He was using a homemade affair—a drum in which, by means of a handle and some apparatus, he whirled a frame of honey, the force sending the sweet stuff flying on to the sides of the drum. The whole atmosphere was charged with the alluring smell. Osborne, crouched in the ditch, sniffed appreciatively.

"I wouldn't mind a feed of that," he whispered to Murphy. "Honey attracts me."

"It attracts other things too," replied Murphy, and as the constable looked at him inquiringly, the sergeant pointed a silent finger to the sky. Jet black against the softer hue of the velvet star-studded heavens, Osborne saw a number of flitting shapes. There must have been two dozen of them. They had stolen up on silent wings and were now circling the old humpy.

"Flying foxes," said Osborne. "Now what the heck are they after? There are no fruit trees around here."

"It's the honey," Murphy explained. "They can smell it."

"But flying foxes don't eat honey, do they?" asked Osborne. "They go for fruit."

"Not always. They like flowers which contain honey or nectar. Some of them go for nothing else, preferring the blossoms of gum and other trees. Others like the fruit of Moreton Bay figs. Spotted gum blossoms are favoured by them all."

"Yes, maybe, but they certainly clean up orchards."

"No doubt about that. But you'll find that they raid orchards when there is a big shortage of their natural food. There are literally millions of flying foxes in Australia, and if they all went after cultivated fruit, there would be none left in no time. All the orchardists would go bankrupt."

"I have an uncle who owns an orchard," said Osborne. "I got a letter from him only last week and he told me that flying foxes are costing him over £30 a week, what with losses of crops and expenses in trying to kill them. He is not the only one. All his neighbors are in the same boat. They patrol their properties every night, shooting flying foxes with double-barrelled guns. They have tried scarecrows, have hung lanterns in the trees, installed electric lights in the orchards and have even organised expeditions to shoot the pests in their camps."

"Ever seen a flying fox camp?" asked Murphy.

"No, but I'd like to."

"The nearest one to this town is fifteen miles away. One of these days I'll take you out there and we'll have some fun. You won't believe it until you see it. Those coves over there doing all the screeching around the Chows' hut have come from that camp."

"They must like long-distance flying," Osborne observed.

"Oh, that's nothing to a flying fox, or to give him his proper name, a fruit bat. The normal feeding area is within a radius of up to twenty-five miles of a camp. Their camps are more or less permanent, too. The one I'm speaking of has been there for over thirty years, according to the old-timers."

"Why don't they get up a party some time and go and clean it out of existence?" Osborne wanted to know.

"Mainly because there are thousands of flying foxes in the camp and ammunition is very costly. Flame-throwers are not much good either. You and I will go out there one of these days and we'll take our shotguns. You'll be able to knock them down from dawn to dusk and you'll never notice the difference in numbers.

"They are useless, destructive animals," he went on, "but interesting all the same. This camp I'm talking about is in a big patch of mangroves over towards the coast. The foxes hang upside down from the branches and from each other, packed in a solid mass. And though they are creatures of the night, the camps during the day are never quiet. The foxes are always fighting and brawling among themselves.

"One of the most interesting sights I have ever witnessed was that camp breaking up. I had been along the coast making some inquiries about a stolen rowing boat, and was on horseback. When I was riding back to town I had to pass close to the flying fox camp, so I pulled up to watch the exodus.

"They didn't just leave the mangroves and fly off independently in all directions. Soon after dusk, they started to move and left in squads, flitting off in different directions in a most orderly manner. There was no hesitating about them. They seemed to know just where they were going. It reminded me of battalions of soldiers marching off to a war, or rather, like squadrons of bombers off to raid some enemy. There were so many of the pests that it took an hour to clear the camp."

"Do they lay eggs like other birds?" asked Osborne interestedly.

"Birds?" snorted Murphy. "Lay eggs? Strike me pink, they aren't birds! Lay eggs, my foot! They are flying mammals and have their young ones like other animals. The youngster clings to its mother by its clawed thumbs and feet and mother takes it on her nightly flights to the feeding grounds until it becomes too heavy Then she leaves it in a secluded spot and brings it fruit and other nice things to eat."

"You must have studied the things in your time, sergeant," commented Osborne.

"I've been around," said Murphy shortly. "You pick up knowledge in all sorts of queer places and I've spent most of my time in the bush."

"I used to have an old aunt—she's dead now, poor old soul—who was scared stiff of flying foxes and the little bats," said Osborne. "She lived in the country and no matter how hot the night might be, she always insisted on closing every window because she was afraid that the little bats would fly in and get tangled up in her hair. She used to insist that bats deliberately tried to settle in the hair of women."

"A lot of women still have that silly idea," grinned Murphy. "It's the battiest thing you ever heard of. As a matter of fact, I've been in rooms when bats have dashed in. What lures them is the insects, particularly moths, mosquitoes and other cooties that have been attracted by the light. The little bats have to be swift and sure when after insects, so it stands to reason that they are agile enough to avoid colliding with people and other objects. Talk about hawks having keen eyesight! Give me a bat every time. Anyway, the little things can't bite or scratch very much and are entirely harmless. Still, lots of people hate the sight of them."

"It probably goes right back to the Middle Ages, or even the Dark Ages," said Osborne. "Remember the old stories of the witches who always used bats' wings for their spells and enchantments? I believe that some of the savage native races in Africa and other parts still use the wing of a bat to warn certain enemies of vengeance due for some crime or other. They nail the wing of a bat to their victim's door and the victim throws double fits, or some such rot. It is all a lot of silly superstition."

"But interesting," said the sergeant. "And most interesting point of all is the fact that the Chinese regard all bats as signs of good luck."

"I'll bet old Hook Suey over there doesn't think much of them at the moment," grinned Osborne. "Those foxes are kicking up the dickens of a row."

And so they were, too. Round and round the humpy they flew, screeching loudly. Once or twice Hook Suey came to the door and looked up solemnly at them, possibly trying to extract some good luck, before going inside to resume his honey separating.

Having finished their discussion on fruit bats, the two watching officers lapsed into silence. Time was beginning to hang heavily on their hands. It was getting late and it seemed as if Wu Wang and Yet Yow would not be returning that night. The screeching fruit bats were getting on the policemen's nerves and they silently cursed them, wishing that they would go away and raid an orchard, preferably one a thousand miles off.

Presently the light in the hut was put out. Apparently Hook Suey was retiring for the night. But as he did not trouble to close the door, which had remained half-open since dusk, the watchers still entertained hopes that the wandering Yet Yow and Wu Wang would come home. While all this was going on, Bill the wombat had been mooching around the gardens, but had not come near the hiding place of the two police officers. The screeching flying foxes over his head did not interest him in the least.

Having investigated a patch of spinach down in a far corner, Bill wandered along the fence on the side of the garden directly opposite to that where Murphy and Osborne were hidden, and presently was nosing along the back of the humpy itself. A fruit case attracted him and he hauled himself up on his two front paws and poked his inquiring nose into it. He was greeted by the smell of some decaying cabbage leaves and after wrinkling his nose in fastidious distaste, dropped to the ground and lumbered around to the front of the hut. He found his way to the partly-opened door and thrust his head tentatively into the aperture. The smell of honey hit him right in the nostrils, but it left him cold. There might, however, be other things inside that would be intriguing.

Giving the door a hard bunt with his head, he sent it open and then slouched into the dark interior. The room, which had hard mother earth for a floor, contained a table, a couple of unstable chairs and a few other odds and ends, including the drum which Hook Suey had been using to separate the honey. Bill examined the whole lot. In a corner he came upon an open bag which contained a few inches of wheat. He took a mouthful, chewed it up and swallowed it. It was good. He took a second mouthful and found that even better. He stayed there until he had eaten all the wheat and then waddled inquisitively through another doorway into an inner room.

This contained a few sticks of furniture and three bunks. The light that filtered through the dirty window which was innocent of curtains showed Bill that two of the bunks were empty. In the third reposed the sleeping figure of Hook Suey. Bill investigated every corner of this room without finding anything he fancied, and then decided to investigate Hook Suey.

Raising himself and placing his front feet on the edge of the bunk, he gazed long and thoughtfully at the sleeping man's face. And as he gazed, the vagrant thought entered his brain that this probably was the mystery monster that had invaded his burrow that morning. So he gave Hook Suey a sudden and violent prod with his nose. Hook Suey grunted, opened his mouth and said a few words in Chinese, shut it again, groaned and turned over on his side, his back towards the wombat. Bill put his head on one side and grunted himself. Then he administered to the Chinese an even more violent prod in the small of the back.

Hook Suey awakened with a start, and turned over, facing the visiting wombat. In the dim light he saw something frightful. Glaring into his eyes and only a few inches from his face was surely the devil himself!

The howl he set up would have scared more than Bill the wombat. That animal gave a terrified snort which turned into a loud and anguished grunt as the Chinese punched him on the nose, knocking him head over heels and landing him on the flat of his back.

Scrambling to his feet, he made for the open air as fast as he could. Hook Suey leaped from his bunk, seized a billet of wood which lay on a small table at the head of the bed, and, howling curses in Chinese, rushed madly after the fleeing wombat.

Bill gained the yard only a few feet ahead of Hook Suey. The Chinese, holding the billet of wood in both hands, made an awful swipe at him. If it had got home, Bill would rapidly have joined his ancestors in the wombats' Valhalla, but it didn't. And so much energy did Hook Suey put behind the blow that, when it missed Bill and hit the ground, he followed it, sprawling full length on hard earth and knocking the wind out of himself.

"What in the name of fortune is going on over there?" exclaimed Murphy in the ditch. "Is somebody getting murdered? It's even scared away the flying foxes."

He and Osborne were sitting on the soft grass on the bottom of the ditch, their heads just protruding over the top and partially screened by the low bush. They could not see anything, but they could hear the pandemonium. In front of them was the wire netting fence.

Murphy was in the act of getting to his feet, the better to see what was transpiring, when some large object loomed up in front of him. There was a sound of smashing wire and the next moment the sergeant received a heavy weight on his chest, knocking him backwards on top of Constable Osborne.

It was Bill the wombat. Having got clear of the hut, the startled Bill rushed straight across the gardens, disdaining to follow paths, and doing quite a bit of damage to vegetable plots. He went through the wire netting as though it were not there, and, unaware of the presence of the two watch-ers—or the deep ditch—was on top of Murphy before he knew it. There was a mad flurry in the ditch as two men and a wombat mixed it up in a brief free-for-all struggle. Osborne was on his back with Murphy sprawled over him, while Bill was on top of the sergeant, sacks-on-the-mill fashion. The wombat was the first to recover himself and, using Murphy as a convenient bridge, treading all over him, scratching his face and putting one hind foot in his mouth, hauled himself from the ditch and lumbered off as fast as he could into the night.

"What on earth happened?" gasped Constable Osborne as they sorted themselves out.

"I'm hanged if I know," groaned Murphy and then broke off with a startled yell as a billet of wood whizzed past his ear, accompanied by a spate of unintelligible language. Hook Suey, following Bill, had reached the fence and, seeing mov-ing figures in the ditch, had taken a chance on their being the "devil" that had invaded his humpy, and had hurled the billet of wood at them.

"Hey, listen, you yellow villain," bawled the sergeant as he again sorted himself out from Constable Osborne. "What do you think you're playing at you yellow coot? Who are you heaving things at? Let me get at you and I'll half-murder you!"

Hook Suey blinked rapidly several times.

"Missa Murphy," he said wonderingly.

"Yes, Missa Murphy," howled the owner of that dis-tinguished name.

"What the heck are you playing at, you yellow coot?"

"Let me get at him, sergeant," exclaimed Osborne irately.

"Missa Osborne," said Hook Suey, completing the iden-tification.

"Yes, Missa Osborne, and I'm going to run you in, you murderer," roared the constable.

"You no dless likee policeman," said Hook Suey, referring to the fact that the two men were not in uniform.

"Never mind about that," said Murphy, getting out of the ditch and climbing through the hole in the wire netting made by Bill. "What's been going on around here? What was that thing that tackled us in the ditch just now? Come on, John, do a bit of explaining."

"Him debbil, him come to hut. Me hunt him away. Thought you debbil in ditch," exclaimed Hook Suey simply.

"Devil? What devil?" exclaimed Murphy impatiently. "I don't know what you are talking about."

Hook Suey slowly explained what he was talking about. He had been sleeping peacefully when he was awakened by a violent blow. In the darkness he saw that it was the devil himself, come to get him for his sins. He had no desire to be taken by the devil, so he had struck it and it had rushed away out of the hut. He had followed it with a billet of wood, but instead of finding a devil he had found two police officers. That was all.

But there was one thing that puzzled the Chinese. "Why you come into hut as devil and frighten Hook Suey?" he asked wonderingly.

"We weren't in your blessed hut, you old goat," said Murphy.

"Why you lie down in ditch like pig?" the Chinese wanted to know.

"Mind your own business," growled the sergeant. "As for your devil, it looked more like a pig. It jumped on me and knocked me flying." He broke off and snorted in disgust.

"Devil? Pig? I might have known it! I'll bet your devil was that darned wombat out on the prowl."

"Lombat?" Hook Suey considered this for a moment or two. "Lombat? Ai. Might have been lombat. Velly sally. No see in dark."

"A fat lot of good this is," said Murphy with another grunt. "The thing scratched my face and put its foot in my mouth. Anyway, I suppose it isn't your fault. All right, John, go back to your nice little bed. I'm going home myself. Come on, Osborne."

As the two policemen, fed to the teeth with their night's adventures, left the Chinese gardens, Bill the wombat entered his burrow up on the slope, his feeling of disgust quite equalling that of the two men. Frankly, he had had enough of these goings-on. Life was just one hectic moment after another. It was too much of a good thing.

And as he curled up in his nest, he reached a momentous decision—he would find another home, far away from the Chinese gardens: a haven of peace where an inoffensive wombat might lead a placid existence.

CHAPTER TEN

A Strange Meeting

THE sun was just thinking of turning in for the night and was creeping tiredly beneath a fleecy blanket of white clouds in the west as Bill left his burrow on the following evening. He did not shed one sentimental tear at the thought of leaving his home. When he had retired that morning it was with the resolve to get out and, having slept on the idea, he still found it a good one when he awakened.

He lumbered purposefully down the slope without a backward glance, turned to the left on reaching level ground, and trotted along until he came to the bank of the creek. Here certain lush grass claimed his attention for some time, and after he had made a moderate meal, he proceeded on his way. There was a well-defined path along the creek bank, used by both animals and humans, and Bill kept up a steady gait until he had travelled perhaps a mile from his old home. This was the first occasion that he had been in this particular area and he took time off from home-seeking to attend to certain succulent roots which he had unearthed.

A track, diverging from the one along the creek bank and leading down to the water's edge, attracted him, and he waddled down it to have a drink. His thirst slaked, he went along the water's edge for a short distance and then decided to climb the sloping bank and return to higher ground.

The spot he selected for his moderate mountaineering was rather steep and when he had scaled three or four feet, he found he could get no higher because of a projecting treeroot. It was too large for him to gnaw through unless he was prepared to spend half the night on the job, so he decided to drop back to the water's edge and try another and easier climbing place.

It was then that he noticed a large hole under the tree root. He inspected it thoughtfully. It appeared to be the burrow of some animal, but the opening was too small for a wombat, unless it happened to be an undersized runt; but Bill knew that there were no other wombats around.

Studying the hole closely, Bill noticed queer marks leading from it—obviously the footprints of its owner. But the wombat had never seen marks like them before.

He had resolved that the matter was no concern of his and was about to retire down the sloping bank, when the strangest creature he had ever seen appeared at the mouth of the hole and stared at him with little beady eyes. It looked like a duck, but it had fur on its head, and Bill could see that its front feet were webbed.

Bill the wombat was not the first living creature to be startled by the appearance of the species of animal now regarding him with great distrust. For well over a hundred years scientific human beings had been puzzling their brains over what made the platypus the way he was. The first natural history experts felt like booking rooms in the nearest lunatic asylum when they saw a creature with a brown fur coat, a duck-like bill and webbed feet, and then discovered that it laid eggs and suckled its young. When the first platypus (dead) was taken to Europe, scientists said that it did not exist—that it had been invented by artful Chinese out of odds and ends of other creatures and sold to simple seamen who did not know any better. When convinced that it did exist, they gave it the title of Ornithorhynchus.

The platypus eyeing Bill the wombat was a female and she was coming out at twilight, as was her custom, to get a bit of fresh air and a meal in the creek below, leaving her two youngsters safe asleep in the nesting chamber at the end of the burrow nearly thirty feet deep in the side of the creek bank. The youngsters were only a few weeks old and the mother platypus had some lost time to make up.

While the eggs had been hatching, she had not left the burrow. Custom demanded that she eat twice a day—at dawn and late in the afternoon. Like the rest of her kinsfolk she spent little more than a couple of hours each day in the water.

The platypus had two homes—one which she shared with her mate in between the breeding seasons, and the breeding burrow itself. This she had built entirely on her own, and in it her husband was as welcome as an onion in a scent factory. He remained in the ordinary, every-day residence and she would not join him again until the young ones were tossed out into the world to make their own livings. But that would not be for some time to come.

About a month before Bill's arrival, the female platypus had tunnelled out her breeding burrow and had made a nest of reeds which she had chewed up and carried inside. When she was ready to lay her eggs, she had retired into the burrow and as she went, had erected barriers of soft earth every four feet or so. These barriers, which she had flattened hard with her tail, were four or five inches thick. She erected them because, though her burrow was well above water-level as was the case with all other platypus homes, a sudden rise in the creek might flood her nest while she was in retirement hatching her eggs. The barriers, too, would keep out undesirable visitors.

The mother platypus had laid two eggs. These had soft shells and were dirty white in color. She had then curled her body around them and had possessed her soul in patience for about ten days. Both eggs had hatched, and she began to suckle the youngsters. She had also left the burrow for the first time since the eggs were laid and had indulged in a record meals of worms, grubs and yabbies, a bountiful supply of which the creek provided. The young ones were now two weeks old and were still sightless. It would be quite another eight or ten weeks before they would be able to see the world for the first time. But their first glimpse of anything would be of the uninteresting interior of the burrow, because their mother would not permit them to have their first swim until they were at least four months old.

The platypus did not know what to make of Bill. If he had never seen her like before, she could return the compliment. She thought of her babies back in the nest and grew nervous, wishing that this unwelcome visitor would go away and leave her alone.

Bill the wombat might not be in the first hundred in an animal beauty contest and he might look grumpy and formidable, but his heart was in the right place. He had no desire to scare or even to inconvenience the platypus. He was just a little curious to know what she was, that was all.

With this end in view, he advanced a little to get a closer look. The platypus, properly alarmed, turned round and vanished down the burrow. Bill thrust his inquisitive nose into the entrance and had a good sniff. That gave him no information. Puzzled, he gave it up as a profitless pastime and scrambled down to the creek edge. Working his way back in the direction from which he had come, he presently found the path he had used to reach the waterfront and by this means regained higher ground.

CHAPTER ELEVEN
News Of The Box

SERGEANT MURPHY was sitting in his room at the police station a few mornings later turning over in his mind the problem of the missing Chinese, Yet Yow and Wu Wang, and of the mysterious yellow box. He was satisfied in his own mind that the two Chinese had found the box in the wombat's burrow and were keeping out of sight with it. But where they were hiding, he had been unable to discover. Thinking that they may have called upon Ling Yuang with it and endeavoured to sell it back to him, Murphy had seen the old Chinese. Ling Yuang had told him with some emphasis that he had had no visitors with yellow boxes, and then had gently chided the sergeant for his failure to find it.

Taking this with that, Sergeant Murphy was not too pleased with life in general, and his frame of mind was by no means made happier when he learned that his fellow police officers and certain others had given him the nickname of "Wombat." That, he guessed, was the work of young Constable Osborne, who had, no doubt, told about their adventure in the ditch outside the Chinese market gardens. He had tackled the constable about it, but Osborne had proclaimed his innocence.

"These things get around," Osborne had said with a chuckle.

Murphy, who had resented that chuckle, had replied that he failed to see how a thing could have gone around when only two persons had known it had happened. He himself had not talked.

"Perhaps the wombat opened his big mouth," laughed Osborne.

For that remark, Murphy had punished Osborne by sending him twenty miles away into the bush to investigate a report of horse stealing.

Across the sergeant's forehead was a wide strip of sticking plaster which covered a deep scratch. This was the work of Bill the wombat, who had used his claws to good effect when turning Murphy into a bridge to get out of the ditch. People had accepted Murphy's explanation that he had got tangled up in a rosebush at his home until somebody, and Murphy knew it was Osborne, had pointed out that the sergeant did not grow roses.

Murphy was still brooding at his desk when Clarence and Herbert burst unceremoniously into his presence. Herbert's eyes still showed faint signs of its acquaintance with Bill the wombat's nose.

"Well, what do you two jokers want?" asked the sergeant curtly. "Incidentally, do you both live in a tent, or don't you usually knock at a door before you enter a room?"

Clarence and Herbert looked at him for a few seconds without speaking. Then,

"You been having a box-on with somebody, Mr. Murphy?" Clarence asked.

"I have not. What gave you that idea?" asked the sergeant.

"Why, the dirty big hunk of sticking plaster on your forehead," said Clarence.

"It is neither big nor dirty," said Murphy testily. Then he gave a faint smile.

"To tell you the truth, boys," he said, "I got it off a wombat. I was lying in a dirty big ditch when this wombat came up suddenly, knocked me flat on my back, shoved its foot in my mouth and scratched my forehead."

Clarence gave a hoarse chuckle and Herbert a loud snort.

"That's right," said Herbert indignantly. "Sling off at me. Go on, chuck dirt. I know I got a black eye when a wombat clouted me in his burrow and nobody will believe me when I tell them. They say some bloke must have punched me. Go on, chuck off a bit more. I like it. So a wombat trod on you and scratched your forehead? Nobody donged you, did they? Oh, no!"

"I'm sorry, Skinny," said Murphy laughing. "I apologise. As a matter of fact, a wombat did not do this to me. I was walking in my garden when I got tangled up in a dirty big climbing rose which made a deep scratch in my forehead."

"Yes, well, why didn't you say so in the first place instead of all this tripe about wombats?" exclaimed Herbert. "And don't call me Skinny! You coppers are always kicking up a fuss because crooks and other blokes won't tell you the truth, yet you tell blessed lies yourselves."

"Herbert, old fellow," said Murphy handsomely, "you are perfectly correct. I accept your rebuff and apologise deeply. Now what did you want to see me about?"

"Have you caught up with them Chows, Yet Yow and Wu Wang, since that day we was at the wombat's burrow?" asked Clarence. "If not, then we know where they are—over at Gull Island."

"That's right," said Herbert. "Me and Clarence was over there yesterday afternoon in a boat, fishing. We saw these two Chows with a third one. They was walking along the beach there."

"At Gull Island? Are you sure it was them?"

"No doubt about it. We know them three Chows at the gardens well," said Clarence. "Many the chase they've given us in the past."

"I'll bet. Did they have the yellow box with them?" asked Murphy.

"No."

"I wonder what the dickens they are doing over there?" pondered the sergeant. "Only about a dozen people all told live on the island. This other Chinese you mention must be hiding Yet Yow and Wu Wang."

"Could be," nodded Herbert, "but they wasn't doing any hiding yesterday."

"Come to that, I suppose there is no real reason why they should be hiding," Murphy said thoughtfully. "After all, they don't know that we suspect they have the stolen box, so why should they hide?"

"You gonna go chase 'em?" asked Clarence.

"I'm gonna do just that little thing," said the sergeant. "And if you two birds have nothing on hand, you'd better come with me. We can hire a launch to go over. It's only a mile and a half, and we'll be back in no time."

"Suits me down to the ground," said Herbert enthusiastically.

"Me too," said Clarence heartily.

It was a three miles drive to the waterfront and Murphy and his young companions made the trip in an old car belonging to Constable Osborne. As Murphy pointed out, Osborne would have no use for it, seeing that he was miles and miles away in the bush hunting horse thieves.

They had no trouble hiring a small launch, the owner of which went with them to drive it. Murphy could have done the job himself, but he raised no objection to the grizzled old fisherman, Ike Pratt, going along.

"You know much about Gull Island?" Murphy asked him as the little launch chugged its way across the calm surface of the inlet.

"Every inch of the place," sid the fisherman. "You gonna run anyone in?" He ran his eye over Murphy's uniform as he asked the question.

"Don't know," said the sergeant. "Just making a few inquiries first. "Do you happen to know if any Chinese live on the island?"

"Yep. Only one. Feller named Nung Sam. Got a bit of a garden, and does a bit of watch-mending and key-cutting and so forth."

"He wouldn't make a fortune out of that, stuck on a small place like Gull Island," observed Murphy.

"Now you'd be surprised about that," replied Ike Pratt. "Plenty of people from the mainland take their watches and clocks to him. They find it cheaper than going to regular jewellers. Nung Sam does it for a hobby and charges only for the cost of spare parts if they are needed."

Murphy fell silent for a moment and idly watched Clarence and Herbert, who were in the stern of the launch trailing a fishing line. He wondered what they hoped to catch. They had no sinker on the line and he could see that the bait, a piece of fatty meat they had picked up on the jetty, was skipping over the water about twenty feet astern.

As he watched, a cheeky silver gull appeared from nowhere and made a grab at the bait. Clarence was holding the line and when he saw the gull, he quickly hauled in the slack.

"Thieving coot," he said sternly. "Get back to your missus and kids on Gull Island."

"How do you know he comes from Gull Island?" asked

Herbert argumentatively. "I'll bet you a quid there ain't any gulls on the place in spite of its name."

"You'd lose your bet, young feller," put in the fisherman. "The place is packed with them and their nests. I'm surprised that kids like you didn't know that. There are hundreds of nests on the ground just in-shore on the other side of the island. The gulls just scrape out a bit of a hole and line it with grass or dried seaweed and they nest so close together it makes you wonder how they find their own homes."

"I must raid 'em some time," said Clarence.

"What for?" asked Ike Pratt. "Useful birds, the gulls. They clean up all the rubbish and stuff in harbours, such as garbage and offal thrown overboard from ships. I've seen 'em eating scraps of tucker left by untidy people having picnics on the beaches."

"Yes, but what do they eat when they can't get that food?" asked Clarence. "There ain't always ships coming in and out of harbours and what about in the winter when people don't have beach picnics?"

"Fish and prawns and insects and so forth," said Old Ike. "They also go the bash on other birds' eggs, such as gannets and terns. Anyway, they don't always stick to the seashore, you know. I've seen 'em myself miles inland on lagoons and waterholes and also in paddocks picking up grubs and worms. Some of them follow the plough on farms just like magpies and peewits, or ordinary chooks."

"Well, what do you know about that!" said Herbert, quite unimpressed.

"All I know is that they are thieving coots," said Clarence, thinking of the piece of bait.

"Coots are different birds altogether," said the fisherman. "They're blue and black coloured and hang around swamps."

He grinned widely. "You reckon seagulls are thieves? Too

right they are. A cobber of mine who gets around told me once that down in Tasmania at a place I forget the name of, the silver gulls there ride on the backs of pelicans and use them as fishing boats. Every time a pelican catches a fish, the gulls dive at it and pinch it before the pelican can swallow it. It doesn't always come off, but the gulls make a good living out of it. Not a bad idea that, using a pelican both as a fishing boat and a fisherman too. It's true, too, because my mate showed me a bit about it in a newspaper."

Clarence and Herbert said nothing to that. Neither did Murphy. For a moment the silence was painful. Old Ike Pratt could see that his passengers did not believe him, but he merely shrugged his shoulders and attended to his steering.

"They are seagulls, anyway," said Clarence, breaking the silence.

"Who said they weren't?"

"You called them silver gulls."

"Same thing. Seagulls or silver gulls. Same bird. There are other gulls, of course, such as the Pacific gull and the skua. The Pacific gull is a proper robber. Big bird, too.

Seagulls are white and Pacific gulls are larger and have yellow beaks with red tips. You don't see many of them in these parts. They are farther south and don't get about in flocks like silver gulls. They like the young mutton birds and their eggs and destroy them in thousands. Pacific gulls can tear young mutton birds to pieces and I've seen 'em do it. Anyway, if you want to study gulls, you go and have a look at their nests on the island. And don't go pinching their eggs."

He lapsed into a reverie and for some moments there was again silence in the boat. They were now more than halfway to Gull Island and the thoughts of Murphy at least were centred in his coming interview with Yet Yow and Wu

Wang—if they were still there.

Arriving at the island, Ike Pratt piloted the launch to a small jetty and tied her up. He said he would do a bit of fishing while awaiting the return of his passengers.

"I might have a couple of extra ones for you," said Murphy grimly.

"Thought you said you wasn't gonna arrest anyone?" said Pratt. "I don't want to be mixed up in any violence with crooks."

"Don't worry about that. If I bring along a couple of extra passengers there won't be any violence. They will not be that type. Anyway, you're being paid for it, ain't you?"

"Yes, but this boat is not a Black Maria or a police patrol van," the fisherman pointed out.

Murphy did not reply to that, but asked Pratt where the watch-repairing Chinese could be found. The fisherman gave him the necessary directions and Murphy, Clarence and Herbert departed.

"Think there will be a brawl, Mr. Murphy?" asked Clarence hopefully. "If so, me and Herbert can help you handle them. One Chow each."

"They might carry knives and pig-stabbers," said Murphy without a smile.

"We've got our shanghais," responded Clarence and then gave a shout of laughter.

"What's biting you all of a sudden?" demanded Murphy.

"Shanghais!" shouted Clarence. "Don't you get it? We're gonna clean up some Chows with shanghais. Chows come from Shanghai. Funny, ain't it, huh?"

"You slay me," said Murphy. "You're wasting your time. You should be on the stage making big money."

"Yep. I've often thought that myself," said Clarence complacently. "I'm pretty good at making up funny things."

"So were your parents," said the sergeant.

"I don't get that," said Clarence gropingly, while Herbert broke into raucous laughter.

"Skip it. This looks like the place we want."

It was a small hut in the middle of a small garden which did not possess a gate. The three visitors walked in and Murphy banged on the door. This was opened by a witheredup Chinese, who blinked at him dubiously.

"I'm a police officer," said Murphy unnecessarily. "Are you Nung Sam?" The Chinese nodded.

"I want to see your two friends, Yet Yow and Wu Wang."

"Not here. Gone home."

"Hey?" exclaimed the sergeant. "When was this?"

"One, two, three hours ago."

"Well, I'll have a look round your hut while I'm here."

"Whaffor? Nung Sam he done nothing!"

Murphy unceremoniously pushed him aside and entered the hut. Clarence and Herbert followed him, each of them giving Nung Sam a most unwarranted shove as they did so. And no sooner were they inside than Clarence gave a cry of exultation.

"There it is, Mr. Murphy—slap bang in the middle of the table!" he cried. "That's the box itself!"

On the table in the centre of the room reposed Ling Yuang's mysterious yellow box. Murphy studied it curiously before he picked it up for a closer inspection.

"So!" he breathed. Then, turning to Nung Sam, who had entered the room, he said briskly, "Where did you get this thing from?"

"Had it long time," said the Chinese. "Bring from China when little boy."

"Why, you thumping old liar!" exclaimed Clarence. "You pinched it."

"Pipe down, you, and let me handle this," instructed Murphy. "You got this box from Yet Yow and Wu Wang, didn't you?"

"Not true," said Nung Sam.

"This box has been stolen and unless you tell me the truth, I'm going to arrest you and take you back to the mainland with me."

"Box stolen?" asked the Chinese warily. "You tellum truth?"

"Yes," said Murphy and told Nung Sam the story of the box—how it had been stolen from Ling Yuang by somebody and how it had come into the possession of Wu Wang and Yet Yow. At the end of the story, Nung Sam nodded slowly.

"Him box, him come from Yet Yow and Wu Wang," he said.

"Why did they bring it here?" asked the sergeant.

The Chinese told him that, like all of his fellow country-men, he had heard of the mysterious box of Ling Yuang, but had never seen it nor heard it described. He had no idea that the box on the table was that very object. Yet Yow and Wu Wang had told him that they had bought it at a second-hand shop. They had been unable to open it without damaging it because of its complicated locking device and they wanted him to do the job for them. Up to date he had not succeeded, although he had tried every means he knew.

"But why did they leave it with you?" asked Murphy. "To be safe. They say velly valuable box. They know I cannot open. They said they come back soon to get." "Why did they stay here for two or three days? Were they waiting to see if you could open the thing?"

"Ai." Nung Sam nodded slowly. "Not tlust me. Want to be here when opened. They give me two pound to keep box safe until they come back to get."

Murphy guessed that Wu Wang and Yet Yow had returned

to the mainland to show themselves and if any questions were asked, they could say that they had been away visiting friends. The box would not be in their possession, even if they were suspected of having it. Anyway, the explanation did not matter much. He had the box and that was the main thing. He could question Wu Wang and Yet Yow on the first occasion he caught up with them.

"I'm taking this box back with me," he told Nung Sam, and departed, Clarence and Herbert, disappointed at the absence of a brawl, followed him moodily.

The fisherman greeted their return with the comment, "No arrests after all!"

"Not this trip," said the sergeant as he climbed aboard the launch. Clarence and Herbert also hopped on board and the fisherman got the engine going and pointed the launch's nose towards the mainland.

"You gonna try to open the box, Mr. Murphy?" inquired Herbert.

"No, I am not. I'm going to take it straight back to the police station and later get old Ling Yuang to identify it. Then I'm going to give it to him and forget all about it."

"What about the cove who pinched it? Aren't you gonna run him in?" asked Clarence incredulously.

"You tell me who it was and then we'll both know," said Murphy.

"Yes, but what about them two Chows who pinched it from the wombat's burrow? You gonna let 'em off free?" exclaimed Herbert, who was thinking about his black eye.

"Don't interfere in police business," said Murphy.

Herbert grunted and shut up.

The return trip to the mainland was made almost in silence. Ike Pratt, reaching his jetty, skilfully guided the craft in and expertly moored her. Murphy clambered ashore and asked Herbert to hand him up the yellow box. Herbert, who was down the stern of the boat, stumbled over the seat in front of him, picked up the box and with a cheerful, "Here she comes!" hurled it at Sergeant Murphy.

Unprepared for the manoeuvre, the sergeant watched the box fly towards him and, describing a graceful curve as it fell short, drop into the water with a great splash.

"Gosh!" said Herbert. Murphy also said something and he did not say it softly.

"Clumsy clot!" he bellowed when he had recovered himself. "Now just you dive straight into that water and get that box back or I'll wring your neck for you."

Herbert peered over the side of the boat. The water was very clear and about ten feet down he could see the yellow box on the sandy bottom, shimmering like gold.

"Go on, in you get. Don't stop there looking at it," shouted Murphy. "Get over and find that box or you'll have another black eye to match the one the wombat gave you."

Herbert closed his eyes and counted ten before he said anything. Then—

"That does it," he said in cold rage. "That is the absolute last straw. First you get me to crawl into a burrow where I get half-killed by a dirty big wombat, and now you want me to go diving into deep water where I'm likely to get bitten in halves by a dirty big tiger shark. I won't, see? I'm hanged if I will. If you want that box you'll get it yourself. Think I want to be bait for a dirty big grey nurse shark?"

"You won't be," put in old Ike Pratt. "It's most unlikely that a grey nurse shark would be around here. Most extremely unlikely. I'm a fisherman and I know."

"There you are," said Murphy. "He knows what he's talking about. Hop in and get that box, do you hear?"

"I hear, but I'm not doing it."

"Now if you had said a whaler shark," continued Pratt, "I would not have corrected you. It is the whaler shark that comes into bays and inlets such as this."

"I don't care what brand of shark it is. The bite is the same. Don't be so dashed clever, you old goat. You get the box for the sergeant. I'm going home and in one piece."

Saying which, he climbed on to the wharf and marched off with never a backward glance. Grunting and snorting, Murphy borrowed a long boathook from Pratt and succeeded after a lot of juggling and prodding in getting the yellow box into shallow water. He then hooked it ashore and took it to the car.

He was not surprised to find Herbert sitting in the back seat with his nose in the air in high disdain. He said nothing and Murphy said less. Reaching the township, Murphy dropped the two lads at a convenient corner and then drove round to the police station.

CHAPTER TWELVE
Bill's New Home

B ILL the wombat excavated his new burrow in a rocky
ridge on a hillside about five miles from his old home.
The country here was not as pleasant and the view was
inferior. From the front door of his former residence, the
wombat had had the delightful vista of an enchanting square
of green in its various tints—the Chinese market garden
and its enticing vegetables. His new burrow overlooked an
expanse of open paddocks bisected by fences and inhabited
by a few horses and cows, with the creek in the distance.

The site of the burrow was not the best, either. The
ground was hard and flinty and gave Bill a lot of tough digging. He drove his tunnel only eight feet and then gave it
up. That would be deep enough, he felt. His nesting recess
was lined with grass and leaves. There were several other
wombats with homes in the same hillside and they were as
unsociable as all the others of his kind that he had ever met.
This suited Bill, who had had enough of company, animal
or human, to last him for a long time.

A few feet from his new burrow mouth, Bill found a
hollowed-out nook under an overhanging rock. The surface
was sandy and he turned it into a sunbath.

Returning home at dawn one morning, he did not immediately make for his nest, but relaxed in the sunbath. He rolled over a few times and then thoughtfully stropped his back against the rock to get rid of a momentary itch. Presently the sun peered over the far horizon, its first brilliant rays infiltrating every nook and cranny of the land and stirring the sleeping world into wakefulness.

There were, however, many creatures that had not awaited the rising sun's warning that it was time to get up. Every hour of daylight was precious and the bush creatures were astir with dawn itself. In particular, the preying hawks and falcons were out before actual daylight, pouncing on birds and other small creatures still too befuddled with sleep to protect themselves or to escape.

But now flocks of little finches were busy among the acacias, brilliant honeyeaters thronged the banksias, and over on the flat a pair of peewits with their sweet "bob-o-link" call had been foraging for food since the earliest light. Sometimes they spoiled their attractive notes by uttering harsh noises which grated on the ears. The paddocks were filled with small bird life. Pipits, ground larks, skylarks, quail and others nested and inhabited the grass tufts and stubble and made good hunting for preying hawks and their kin.

The peewits had built their mud nest in a gum tree on a limb projecting over a waterhole in one of the paddocks. On the branch below was a willy wagtail's nest. This was as it should be. No self-respecting peewit would nest in a tree that did not contain a wagtail's home. Maybe it was the other way round. But all the bush creatures knew and accepted the fact that where there was a peewit's nest, invariably a cheeky willy wagtail lived close by.

The peewits were the hungriest birds in the whole district. From the first peep of dawn until the darkness made it impossible for them to see properly, they hunted for food. There was not much else for them to do. Being among the worst fliers in birdland, they could not indulge in long exploratory trips like the great wedge-tailed eagles, or even the small swallows. They could not perform aerial acrobatics like willy wagtail, or shoot like feathered bullets through trees and scrub after the manner of the honeyeaters and little parrots.

When the peewits did any flying, they had a definite purpose in view. They wanted to get somewhere, so usually flew in a straight line, clumsily flapping their wings as if it were hard work. Willy wagtail used to take an insulting delight in performing in front of the peewits, darting this way and that and sometimes looping the loop like a crazy aeroplane pilot. It did not impress the peewits, but Willy thought it did, and no harm was done.

But though the black and white birds were no great shakes as fliers, they were excellent walkers and spent more time on the ground than in the air. With their long, graceful, stilt-like legs, they were continually on the move, searching for fresh water snails, insects and other creatures in green or swampy places, and doing a remarkably good job for the farmers as well as for themselves. These fresh water or pond snails that the birds loved so much, were hosts for a flat worm parasite known as a liver fluke. This wog, when it developed, left the snail and took to the water. Sheep, drinking the water, swallowed the fluke, which attacked its liver, causing serious loss among the woolly animals.

The paddock in which the peewits and their friend willy wagtail lived was a favorite hunting ground for birds of prey, and if Bill the wombat, lazing in his sunbath, had been more observant, he would have seen much to interest him. For instance, there were two spotted swamphawks, or harriers, which spent most of their time prospecting the grass and stubble for small birds, lizards, field mice and the like. They kept to the air a great deal, not like their kinsfolk, the brown hawks, who sat around on fences or in trees, using their eyes to comb the landscape for birds, mice, grasshoppers, beetles and caterpillars. They never caught their prey on the wing, but pounced on it while it was on the ground. The harriers grabbed their meals out of the air or on mother earth. It was all the same to them.

Frequent visitors to the paddocks were two black falcons, real robber birds, who hunted all the others, either to kill them for food, steal their prey, or both. The falcons went for anything and everything, but, in particular, they did love quail.

On this morning that Bill the wombat was lazing in his sand hole, a black falcon was hovering over the field keeping an eye out for quail. There were a few of these in the thick grass and whether they knew a falcon was abroad or not, they kept close to the ground. But when one of them commenced to creep through the stubble, the falcon sighted it. The quail was moving slowly and taking every advantage as to cover, but the keen-eyed falcon followed its movements with ease. He knew that if the quail took to the air, he would have to be quick to seize it, because the ground bird would fly only a short distance and at a great pace.

Something must have startled the quail or it was sick of creeping through the stubble, for it did take to the air. Like an arrow, the falcon was after it, but before he could secure the prey, the quail had dropped back to ground and had burrowed into a big patch of tufty grass out of which the falcon had little hope of dragging it.

Disgruntled, the falcon flew off and perched on the highest branch of a dead tree, and then became rather annoyed to observe a kestrel, or sparrow-hawk, hovering over the spot where the quail had taken refuge. The falcon was trying to make up his mind whether he should tackle the kestrel and drive it away, when a brown hawk appeared from somewhere and took to the kestrel in midair. There was a lot of cackling and chattering and a flurry of feathers and then the kestrel departed in a hurry, leaving his brown relation to prospect the tufty grass to find out what had been the attraction.

From his lookout in the dead tree, the falcon saw the brown hawk suddenly plunge to earth and then rise with something in its talons. The falcon did not wait to ponder on what the hawk had secured, but went for him with great speed. The brown hawk, surprised, dropped its small burden which the swooping falcon retrieved before it struck the ground. It was a small ground lark which had been nesting under a tuft of grass near to where the quail had landed. That wily bird had not stayed long in the tufty growth, but had made for the safety of some bunchy vegetation nearby.

It was sheer bad luck for the lark that the quail should have landed so close to its nest and thus attracted successively a falcon, a kestrel and a brown hawk. The lark, a female, had been brooding on her four freckled eggs in her cup-shaped nest of grass which was partly protected by overhanging vegetation, but it had not escaped the sharp eyes of the hunting brown hawk.

Having stolen the lark from the brown hawk, which did not attempt to get it back again, the falcon returned to the dead tree and quickly had a meal. Then it spent a few minutes hovering over the productive patch in the hope of again flushing the quail, or one of the quail's relations, but had no luck.

Disappointed, it flew across and perched in the tree near

the waterhole—the tree containing the nests of willy wagtail and the peewits. The latter were abroad foraging as usual, but Willy was at home and he greeted the falcon's arrival with a shrill stream of abuse. The falcon took no notice of him, neither did it pay any attention to the peewits which, attracted by the wagtail's protestations, returned hurriedly from their foraging to see what was going on.

The plucky little black and white birds, assisted, or rather, hampered by Willy, who insisted on flying around and making a terrific noise, attacked the falcon together. The falcon, which in favourable circumstances, could have killed the whole three of his antagonists in three fell swoops, yawned a little, and then flew away. He was rather a mild-tempered bird as falcons go, which was really good luck for willy wagtail. Had he been quick to take offence, he would have murdered the wagtail for the insults the little bird hurled after him. Willy's cry of "sweet pretty creature" was particularly offensive, because obviously he did not mean it.

The sun was now high in the heavens and back in the hills, Bill the wombat was feeling very tired and very sleepy. It was time he sought his bed in his burrow, and he was lazily turning the thought over in his mind when he received a strange visitor. This was a large goanna—five feet of it. It came ambling round a corner and when it sighted Bill it poked out its long tongue and hissed threateningly. The goanna appeared to be annoyed about something.

Bill did not get the drift of things. He was doing nobody any harm, just lying there in a sandy hollow, and he could not see why goannas should come along and hiss at him for nothing.

The big reptile was annoyed because he was hungry and because he had just had a great disappointment. Higher up in the hills, the movements of a pair of galahs in a gum tree had told the goanna that they had a nest there. He had seen them going in and out of the hollow end of a dead limb and certain cries he had heard had told him that the galahs had nestlings. A couple of baby galahs would be just the thing to keep a goanna's body and soul together until he found something else.

So the goanna had climbed the tree in his usual fashion-going round and round the trunk like a corkscrew, slowly spiralling upwards until he was within six feet of the hollow limb. There he received a check—the bark had been stripped from the trunk and he could not get a claw-hold on the smooth surface above. This was the work of the wily galahs which, like all their nesting relations, always ringbarked their home tree to trick marauding lizards, tiger and native cats and such ground-living nest robbers.

The goanna tried his best to negotiate the last few feet, but he could not do it. Then, to make matters worse, the galahs spotted him and with shrill cries which rang out far and wide, took to him with their strong beaks and wings, pecking and buffeting him until he was glad to get back to earth again. Even when he was on the ground the indignant birds gave him a torrid time, belting at him until he was glad to run into a hollow log for refuge.

Venturing forth when the coast was clear the goanna pondered deeply on where he could earn a feed quickly and easily. Then he remembered something. Not so long ago he had observed a female goanna laying her eggs in a certain spot not far away. At the time, this natural event had not been noteworthy, but now the memory of the incident caused the big lizard to lick his lips. A bit of a cannibal like most of his kinsfolk, the goanna decided to go and dig up those eggs and eat them.

One, possibly, may sympathise with the big fellow in his

surprise and annoyance when he arrived at the spot to find a wombat calmly lying right on top of the buried eggs! This was a nice state of affairs!

The goanna raised himself on his front feet and hissed and blew at Bill, who looked at him with vague suspicion. The wombat was half asleep and blinked lazily at his visitor. How could he know that he had selected for his sunbath the very place where, some days previously, a female goanna had excavated a hole in the sand, had laid her eggs, covered them up again and left them there to hatch?

Bill had been ready to leave his sunbath and retire to bed, but he certainly was not going to do so now. If he got up and departed, this cheeky-looking goanna would think that he was afraid of it, and that would never do. So Bill, now wide awake, just lay there and allowed the goanna to hiss, blow and poke his tongue out as much as he desired.

The big lizard was getting hungrier and hungrier, but did not know how he could shift the wombat. He waddled close to Bill and glared right into his face. Bill glared back and, thrusting out his head suddenly, bunted the goanna on the nose. The reptile gave back a pace and indulged in a little more hissing, this time like an angry kettle.

Then he decided to act. Creeping close to Bill, he suddenly swung round and struck the wombat a vigorous blow with his large, muscular tail. The blow hurt, and Bill acknowledged the fact with a startled grunt. He got to his feet and charged the goanna, who whirled round and bolted for his life, displaying a swiftness and agility that astonished the wombat. Bill came to a halt and watched the goanna disappear behind some rocks. Then, with a triumphant air, he trotted to his burrow, entered it and bedded down for the day.

As for the cunning old reptile, it, having succeeded in

its objective of luring Bill from the sandy patch, poked its
head around the rocks to make certain that the wombat
had departed. Having satisfied itself on that score, it made
a rush for the sunbath and, quickly unearthing the eggs,
which were six or seven inches below the surface, gobbled
them one after the other. There had been eight eggs in the
"nest," and that, the goanna felt, was a meal which would
keep him going for several hours.

CHAPTER THIRTEEN
The Thieves Are Caught

SERGEANT MURPHY sat in his office at the police station, staring at the yellow box on the table in front of him. It was two days since he had recovered it from Gull Island and he was still ignorant of its contents and of the identity of the persons who had stolen it. He had interviewed Yet Yow and Wu Wang and had told those Oriental gentlemen a few personal things about themselves, adding a dark threat that they would hear from him again later. They had not appeared to be disturbed by that.

Murphy arose from his chair with a sigh and was putting on his uniform tunic when the sound of scuffling and loud voices in the street outside claimed his attention. There seemed to be an argument in progress. He recognised the voice of Constable Osborne.

Going to the front door, the sergeant saw the constable endeavoring to keep two belligerent citizens from fighting each other. One was a little rat of a man and the other a tough individual with a mean face. Catching sight of Murphy, Osborne called out, "Lend a hand with these two bright customers, sergeant. I'm going to run them in for fighting in the street."

Murphy grinned and then grabbed the rat-like man by the coat collar and led him into the police station. Osborne followed with the other.

"What's all the trouble about?" asked Murphy. "What have Hedge and McGinty been up to now?"

"I was coming down the street just now," said Osborne, "and I saw McGinty come out of a shop. Hedge was passing and as soon as he saw McGinty he took to him. There was skin and hair flying for a few seconds until I parted them."

"What is it all about, Hedge?" asked the sergeant curiously.

"Mind your own business," snapped Hedge.

"What have you been up to, McGinty?" Murphy asked, giving the rat-like man a good shaking. "I haven't seen you around town for a spell. Been having a holiday?"

"Too right he has, and on my money, too, the little thief," broke in Hedge.

"The pot calling the kettle black, huh? What did McGinty steal from you, Hedge?"

"Didn't I tell you to mind your own business?" yelled Hedge. "This is a private matter and we'll settle it ourselves."

"I never pinched nothing from you, Dan," whined McGinty. "I wouldn't steal off my best cobber, Dan."

"You'd pinch your grandmother's false teeth, McGinty!" Hedge declared with a sneer. "What happened after I left you that night? It's a funny thing that when you disappeared, the box went too. Very funny."

"What box?" asked Murphy softly.

"No box, at least, just a box of clothes I had in my room, which McGinty sent off."

"Never laid eyes on it, Dan," whined McGinty.

"So," said Murphy, speaking slowly and thoughtfully, "it was you, Hedge, who shoved that box in the waterhole, was it?"

"What box? What waterhole?" demanded Hedge. "I don't know what you are talking about."

"The waterhole in the quarry where you hid the yellow box you stole from Lin Yuang," said the sergeant. A sudden gasp from McGinty made Murphy shoot a quick glance at him. The little rat-like man was gazing at him with wide eyes and open mouth.

"Ah," he said. "Now I see it! It was you, McGinty!"

"I deny it!" screamed the little man. "I didn't shove any box in any waterhole."

"Here, wait a minute," interrupted Hedge. "What is all this about?"

"The whole town knows that Ling Yuang's famous yellow box has been stolen," said Murphy, secretly delighted at the way his chance shots were getting results. "The police recovered it from that waterhole in the quarry and your friend McGinty was seen putting it there one night."

"It wasn't me at all, Dan," bleated McGinty like a terrified sheep. "I don't know how it got into the waterhole. This copper is telling lies."

"So that is what happened to the box, hey?" snarled Hedge. "You sneaked back and took it and hid it in a waterhole. No wonder I couldn't find it when I went back to get it. Now I know why you left town in a hurry. I'd like to cut your throat for you."

"You'd be better employed telling me what this is all about," said Murphy sternly.

"I'll tell you all right," said Hedge between his teeth. "That bright little beauty there pinched the box off old Ling Yang and sold it to me. I hid it and McGinty knew where. Nobody else did. When I went back to get it it had gone. Apparently you found it in a waterhole. That little rat McGinty put it there and then skipped out of town."

"Don't you believe him, sergeant," screamed McGinty in terror. "He pinched the box. He broke into the Chow's shop and took it. I'll get even with him, trying to blame me. We both pinched it and hid it in that old hut in the bush. I admit that I later got it and put it in the waterhole. Yes, I was gonna to stick to it. I don't care now. He tried to put me in. Well, we'll go in together."

"You bet you will," said Murphy in grim agreement. After Hedge and McGinty had been safely locked up in the cells, Murphy and Osborne had a short conference.

"What are you going to do about Wu Wang and Yet Wow?" the constable inquired.

"Well, we have the two actual thieves and that should do us," said Murphy. "We could probably get a case against the two Chinese, but why worry? Personally, I'm glad that the matter is concluded. It has been an irritating affair."

"And a little painful, too," mused Osborne.

"How do you mean?"

"Oh, nothing much," said the constable with a grin. "After all, though, some of us did get ripped about the face by rose bushes and wombats, didn't we?"

"Get out before I throw you out!" roared Sergeant Murphy, and Constable Osborne got out, laughing heartily.

CHAPTER FOURTEEN

The Secret of the Box

WALKING down the street with Constable Osborne one afternoon about a fortnight later, Sergeant Murphy was in a sunny mood. Under his arm he carried the mysterious yellow box and the two officers were returning it to Ling Yuang. That morning, the criminals, Hedge and McGinty, had each been sent to gaol for two years for having broken into his shop and stolen his box. No action had been taken against Yet Yow or Wu Wang. The police had decided to forget about their part in the affair.

Old Ling Yuang greeted his visitors with grave courtesy and invited them into his best room. He asked them to be seated and inquired if they would like refreshment. A cup of tea, he thought, would be nice. Murphy and Osborne replied that it would be nice indeed.

Over the cups of steaming beverage, Murphy told Ling Yuang the complete story of the box's adventures since it had been stolen, even the episode of the wombat's burrow and how he had been scratched by the animal while keeping a watch on the Chinese gardens. He added that the case was finished and he had called to return the box to its rightful owner. The old Oriental thanked him gravely and, taking the box, laid it reverently upon a deep red cushion reposing on a small bamboo table.

Murphy itched to ask Ling Yuang what the box contained, but knew that it would be useless. Instead, he strongly urged the Chinese to keep it in a safe place in future.

"It will be safe, I assure you, Mr. Murphy," said the Chinese. "Now that everything has ended satisfactorily, I should like to make you a small present for all the trouble it has caused you."

"That will not be necessary," said the sergeant. "I am paid to do a job and that is all there is to it. Thanks very much, Ling, but I must decline."

The old Chinese bowed his head understandingly, but both Murphy and Osborne could see that his feelings had been hurt a little. He wanted to show his gratitude, but neither of the policemen could consent to accept presents for duty done.

Then Constable Osborne got a brainwave.

"Say, how about the three of us taking a ticket in the State Lottery?" he suggested. "They say the Chinese are lucky and we have been mixed up with a number of them in this case. What do you say?"

"Suits me fine," said Murphy. "What about you, Ling?"

"Only if you will permit me to buy the ticket," said the Chinese. "Should there be a prize, it shall be divided into three equal parts."

As the idea seemed to delight the old man, Murphy and Osborne agreed readily.

"What will we call the syndicate?" asked Osborne. "China-man's Luck?"

"You wish me to select a name?" asked Ling Yuang, and when both men nodded, the old Chinese looked at Osborne and then at Murphy and the whole of his face lit up in a rare smile.

"I have a good name for it," he said. "A suitable title which you will both like."

"Yellow Box?" asked Murphy carelessly.

"No," said Ling Yuang very gravely. "Wombat!"

"Most appropriate," commented Constable Osborne.

"Extremely so," said Sergeant Murphy between his clenched teeth.

* * *

There was great excitement in the township when the news came through that Ling Yuang, Murphy and Osborne, with the "Wombat Syndicate" had won first prize in the N.S.W. State Lottery. As may be imagined, a lot of fun was poked at the sergeant and there were many sly references to wombats and climbing roses, the story having long since become public property. Murphy, however, the richer by £2,000, his third share, could afford to ignore the insults.

Murphy was a bachelor and lived alone in a small cottage in the centre of the town, and on the night following the news of the lottery win, he was relaxing over a pipe and a newspaper, when there was a knock at the door. His surprise was intense when he opened it to see Ling Yuang. He invited the old man to come in and told him that he was vastly welcome.

"I will not take up much of your time, Mr. Murphy," he said. "It is a cold night and I do not keep late hours." He sat down in the chair indicated by the sergeant and for a while did not speak. He seemed lost in a reverie. Then—

"Mr. Murphy," he began, "I want to tell you the story of the yellow box and to reveal to you a great secret. The time has arrived when I may gratify your understandable curiosity about it."

"Don't worry about that, my friend," said the sergeant.

"It is entirely your own business and I should never have tried to force your confidence. There is no need for you to tell me anything that you might prefer to keep to yourself."

"You have always been a kind and considerate officer," said the old man. "I shall tell you the story and I shall tell it of my own free will."

But Ling Yuang did not seem to be in a great hurry to commence. He brooded for several minutes before he began to speak...

It was the story of his partnership with Wong Sue in the market garden thirty years previously—the story of the disastrous fire that had destroyed their hut and all of Ling Yuang's possessions, including his tiny son. Ling Sen, the baby, had been the apple of his father's eye, but the Fire Gods in their infinite wisdom, had decided that the child should not grow to man's estate.

Old Ling Yuang told the deeply interested sergeant how he and Wong Sue had sold the gardens to Yet Yow, Wu Wang and Hook Suey, and how he had retired to his laundry while Wong Sue had gone to Northern Australia to make his fortune. He told of the pact between them concerning the yellow box—that when Wong Sue returned to China it was to go with him.

"Thirty years have passed and gone and I have heard nothing of Wong Sue," he said. "He is, I am now convinced, dead. He cannot take the box to China for me, so, Mr. Murphy, I shall go with it myself."

"Hey!" exclaimed the sergeant in amazement. "You? Why?"

"It is my desire that the yellow box and what it contains shall rest in the land of my ancestors," said the old Chinese. "I have been a poor man and I have had little desire to accumulate wealth. But now wealth has been thrust upon me by the win in the lottery. I shall travel to China as soon as I can arrange it, and the box goes with me."

He stopped speaking and Murphy remained in deep silence. He was content to allow Ling Yuang to complete his story in his own time.

"I saved very little from that fire thirty years ago, Mr. Murphy, said Ling Yuang slowly. "All was ashes, but from those very ashes I won something infinitely more precious to me than all the gold in the world. There was not much of it—just ashes—but what there was is now in my yellow box, which has never been opened since that day. It will never be opened again. It cannot be. There is no key. Not now. Need I say any more?"

Sergeant Murphy shook his head dumbly. Into his mind there had flamed a great, awakening light. Silently he put out his hand in a token of friendship and understanding. The old man shook it. Then he rose from his chair and moved to the door. Opening it, he paused on the threshold.

"Good-night, my friend. May the blessings of the gods be your always," he said, and the door closed softly behind him.

For a long while Murphy gazed into the heart of the fire, his thoughts with the old Chinese and his yellow box, soon to leave for his native land where the ashes of his beloved son, Ling Sen, would find their last resting place.

CHAPTER FIFTEEN

Bill Comes Home

BILL the wombat emerged from his burrow as the light began to fade and shadows to gather in the nooks and crannies of the hills. The moon hung low in the sky, lifeless, like an orange Chinese lantern that had not yet been lighted.

The wombat was restless and unhappy. He knew he wanted something, but could not determine just what it was. Mooching along with his head down and his shoulders hunched, he made his way aimlessly around the side of the hill and then descended to level ground. He did not pause even to nibble the grass or dig for roots, but ambled along in a dream until he reached the creek. Having had a drink, he wandered along the water's edge for a short distance and then, regaining the higher bank, proceeded a few hundred yards before stopping dead in front of a huge tree stump. He stopped dead by instinct, because he had not seen the stump. Another few inches and he would have banged into it with his thick skull.

He shook his head as if to clear away the cobwebs, and the action must have had the desired effect, because he suddenly knew what he wanted—his old burrow and the Chinese gardens. He had covered half the distance in his aimless wanderings, but now that he had a definite object in view, he broke into a shambling trot. This he kept up intermittently until he reached his destination.

Bill had a free run of the gardens that night. The three Chinese kept strictly to their hut, which was in darkness. Nor did they give any indication of their being at home when the wombat, in the course of his explorations, blundered round the side of the hut and knocked over a kerosene cue which was standing against a wall. The box had a pot plant on top of it, and when Bill barged into it, the pot fell and crowned him, causing him to utter a startled grunt. Then he got tangled up in a roll of wire netting that the Chinese had left lying on the ground, and finished his chapter of accidents by falling into a ditch that Hook Suey had dug as drainage for a new vegetable bed he was planning. This ditch was only a foot deep, but the series of mishaps ruffled Bill so much that he was in no good humour when, at the first hint of dawn, he made his way towards his old burrow up the slope.

And when he reached it, his feelings were by no means soothed by the discovery that, during his absence, another wombat had taken it over.

Fresh signs around the mouth of the burrow told Bill that the interloper was either then actually in residence or was not far away. Seething with indignation, he entered the tunnel and began cautiously to explore it, and when he got to his old nesting chamber and found another wombat curled up there asleep, his exasperated grunt echoed to the very tunnel mouth.

His first impulse was to charge the intruder and have it out with him there and then. It was a trifle hard that a wombat could not go away for a few weeks without some thieving kinsman annexing his home. Bill did not stop to consider the other's viewpoint—that the burrow had been deserted and therefore should not be allowed to go to waste.

Bill fought down his primary impulse to decide the issue on the spot, and substituted strategy. There was no room in the nesting chamber or the tunnel for a fight. It might be possible for him to jump on top of the sleeping interloper and crush the life out of him where he lay in slothful slumber, but that would be awkward and embarrassing. He did not want a dead wombat cluttering up the place and removal of the body would be impossible.

Having worked all this out in his own way, Bill proceeded to put the first part of his plan into action—he woke the other wombat by bunting him forcibly with his head and then giving him a hard shove with both front paws.

Rudely wakened, the intruder blinked dazedly at Bill for a few seconds, wondering what was going on. Bill, narrowly inspecting his unwelcome visitor, saw a young male wombat of goodly size slowly becoming indignant as the meaning of all this penetrated his brain. The youngster had arrived in the district a few days after Bill had departed and, having found a deserted burrow in good order and condition, had saved himself the trouble of digging one by taking it over.

He got to his feet and had a good look at Bill. What he saw did not make him too happy. Bill was full grown and powerful, and would be a holy terror in a fight. The youngster did not want to fight, but he did want to keep the burrow; so he guessed ruefully that if it meant a fight to confirm his occupancy, then it would have to be a fight. But how on earth were they going to battle in the narrow confines of the disputed residence? Perhaps if he were to sit tight in the nest, the newcomer would go away.

While he was debating all this in his mind and keeping a rather fearful eye on Bill, that sagacious creature put the second part of his plan into operation by suddenly cringing back and away. The youngster noted this with surprise and pleasure. So the big chap was afraid of him after all, eh? Good thing!

Bill turned and trotted a few feet and then looked round. The youngster, following him up, paused as Bill grunted menacingly. He backed a few more feet but the youngster did not move. Bill faced the entrance again and waddled a yard or two. Then he paused to listen. Yes, the other wombat was following him cautiously.

Bill's plan was to lure the youngster into the open air and, once outside, with the whole world in which to manoeuvre, he intended to discuss the theft of the burrow with him in no uncertain terms. But this luring game needed great cunning. He did not want the other wombat to think he could get rid of him easily, because the intruder might return to the nest, satisfied that Bill was gone. Bill had to get him out into the open.

Within a few feet of the burrow mouth, Bill paused and waited until the youngster was close to him and then, turning suddenly, made a rush at him and bit him on the nose. The youngster gave a sharp grunt of pain and tried to bite Bill, but that wily old-timer had already backed clear.

And then, as the youngster made a lumbering lunge at him, Bill gave a well-acted whinny of fear and trotted right outside. After him in triumph rushed the other, and when he was actually clear of the burrow, the cunning Bill dodged round the back of him and blocked the tunnel mouth with his body.

There was one thing and one thing only now. If the youngster wanted the burrow, he would have to get rid of Bill and that meant a battle. He measured Bill with his rather inexperienced eye and what he saw did nothing to give him confidence. Bill was ready for fight—actually eager for it—and with his apology for a tail stuck into the entrance of the burrow, he watched his young antagonist's every move. Not that there was much to watch, for the youngster just stood there like a thing frozen.

Then Bill acted. He lowered his head and charged like an angry bull. The younger wombat was unprepared, and received Bill's blunt skull in the chest, the impact throwing him back on to his haunches. Raising himself on his hind legs, Bill brought both his front paws crashing down, his shovel-like nails ploughing two furrows through the fur on either shoulder. The young wombat did not like this at all, and endeavoured to get at Bill with his own claws, but the older animal reared up again and this time gave him such a push that he went head over heels and came to rest flat on his back.

Bill commenced to use the youngster as a doormat, walking and stamping all over him. Bill was a heavy animal and his poor kinsman had all the wind crushed out of him by the time Bill took time off for a short rest. He stood aside and waited until the young wombat regained his feet and then calmly knocked him down again. Then, as a precaution, he lumbered over to the burrow and stood in front of the mouth just in case the youngster should try to sneak into it.

This precaution, however, was unnecessary. The young wombat had had more than sufficient. Under Bill's critical yet wary eye, he examined himself as well as he could and, having reached the rather melancholy conclusion that, though he was still sound enough, he would have a few scars to cherish for quite a time, he trotted away disconsolately.

The triumphant Bill watched him until he was out of sight and then retired to his old sunbath for a short period of sentry duty. He stayed there for half an hour and then, satisfied that the young thief had had enough and would not return again, he entered the old familiar burrow.

Waddling proudly down the tunnel, he relapsed into the nest with a snort of the deepest satisfaction. For the first time in many weeks he was perfectly happy and had not a single care in the world.

With a grunt of profound contentment, Bill the wombat fell asleep.

THE END